PLAY BETTER
GOLF
with
Hale Irwin
edited by Keith Mackie

To my family, especially my wife
Sally for her patience and
encouragement.

This edition published in 1990 by
The Hamlyn Publishing Group Limited,
a part of Reed International Books,
Michelin House,
81 Fulham Road,
London SW3 6RB

ISBN 0 600 57200 5 (hardback)
ISBN 0 600 56792 3 (paperback)

Produced by Mandarin Offset
Printed and bound in Hong Kong

Throughout this book the instructional information is
directed towards and illustrated by the right handed
golfer. Left handed players need to make the necessary
reversal.

Contents

Introduction

The game of golf is littered with instructional gimmicks, instant remedies and 'new' theories, which are like mending a broken golf club with pieces of chewing gum. There is no short cut to lasting improvement at golf, but what I have tried to do in this book is to make it possible for golfers of all ages and ability to understand their own problems. This understanding is the first and most important step towards improvement.

The one essential requirement is honesty. If you fail to apply this quality to the self-analysis section of the book you will be cheating yourself of the best results in the following weeks and months. To fulfil your full potential for improvement will require application and practice—but the results will be lasting because you will have a permanent understanding of the game which will never let you down. You will not find this book full of new swing theories or instant cures. What you will find is a realistic reassessment of the game's fundamental principles based on my years of tournament experience and a close study of the problems which cause most difficulties for amateur golfers.

It is not just the physical side which is important in this game. In fact the mental aspects can be even more vital. There is no reason why the higher handicap player cannot match the better golfer in this area, eventually improving his own standards as a result.

We have tried to present this book in concise and graphic terms with the help of excellent illustrations by George Stokes and photography by Harry Ormesher. I would also like to thank Keith Mackie for his help in the planning and writing of this book, in translating our conversations and thoughts into the words and illustrations which I hope you will find so helpful in improving your golf.

In the following pages I will be guiding you through the mental and physical aspects of golf as though I was standing behind your shoulder like a bad conscience.

At the end of our partnership I hope you gain much more pleasure from your golf by playing a better game.

Hale Irwin

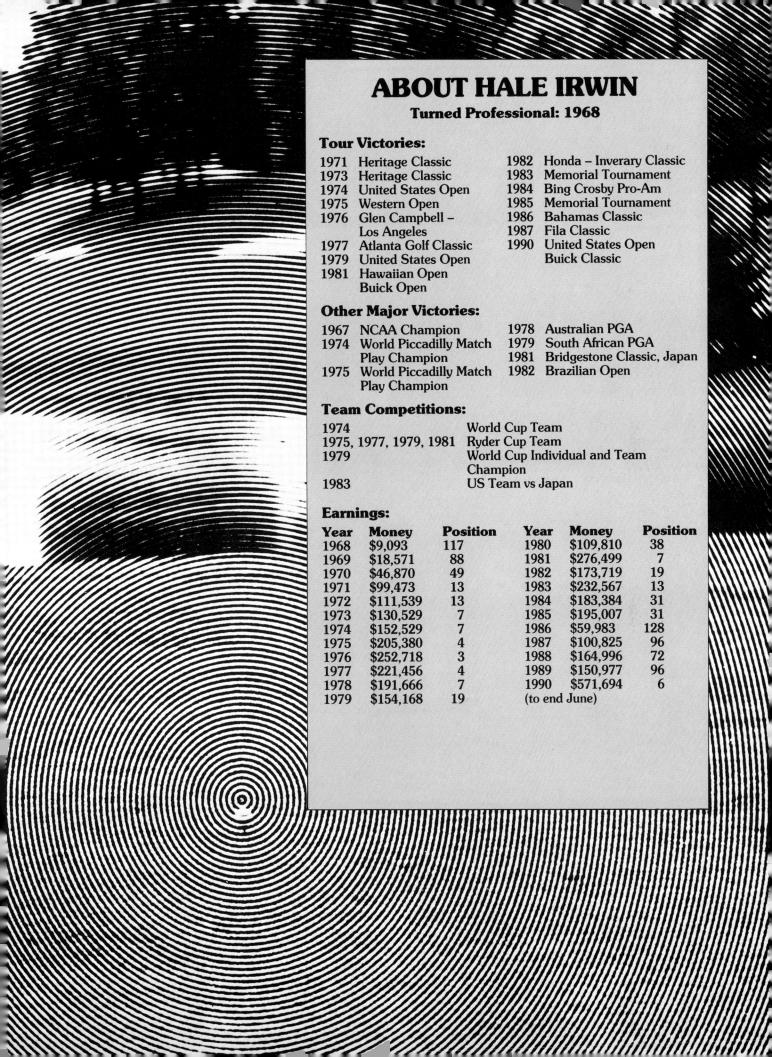

ABOUT HALE IRWIN
Turned Professional: 1968

Tour Victories:

1971	Heritage Classic	1982	Honda – Inverary Classic
1973	Heritage Classic	1983	Memorial Tournament
1974	United States Open	1984	Bing Crosby Pro-Am
1975	Western Open	1985	Memorial Tournament
1976	Glen Campbell – Los Angeles	1986	Bahamas Classic
1977	Atlanta Golf Classic	1987	Fila Classic
1979	United States Open	1990	United States Open
1981	Hawaiian Open Buick Open		Buick Classic

Other Major Victories:

1967	NCAA Champion	1978	Australian PGA
1974	World Piccadilly Match Play Champion	1979	South African PGA
1975	World Piccadilly Match Play Champion	1981	Bridgestone Classic, Japan
		1982	Brazilian Open

Team Competitions:

1974	World Cup Team
1975, 1977, 1979, 1981	Ryder Cup Team
1979	World Cup Individual and Team Champion
1983	US Team vs Japan

Earnings:

Year	Money	Position	Year	Money	Position
1968	$9,093	117	1980	$109,810	38
1969	$18,571	88	1981	$276,499	7
1970	$46,870	49	1982	$173,719	19
1971	$99,473	13	1983	$232,567	13
1972	$111,539	13	1984	$183,384	31
1973	$130,529	7	1985	$195,007	31
1974	$152,529	7	1986	$59,983	128
1975	$205,380	4	1987	$100,825	96
1976	$252,718	3	1988	$164,996	72
1977	$221,456	4	1989	$150,977	96
1978	$191,666	7	1990	$571,694	6
1979	$154,168	19	(to end June)		

Know your game

Over the years golf instruction has become so involved that most players totally overlook the beautiful simplicity of the basic concepts. I am starting here with an explanation of the causes of various types of shot.

An understanding of the fundamental factors which cause certain reactions in the swing and therefore affect the behaviour of the ball is critical in any attempt to produce free-flowing shots which land the ball on target. Given the right information every golfer is capable of analysing his own swing.

Let's get to know each other a little better—because we are going to be spending quite a lot of time together over the next few months. If you accept what I said in the introduction to this book then I am going to be right alongside you every time you hit a golf shot, every time you step on the practice ground, every time you sit quietly at home and think back over your last game or look forward to the next.

In the beginning
We can start the process that will make you a better golfer almost anywhere just so long as you have a few minutes to devote some thought to your game. It can be sitting in your favourite armchair, while you are getting bored or frustrated in a traffic hold-up, between appointments at the office, during a flight or while waiting at an airport—or at home washing the dishes.

Let me start by telling you a little about my game and then we can see how it compares with yours. Basically I'm a fairly orthodox player who believes that golf can be played with a variety of individualistic styles—but there are certain ground rules, basic, unchangeable fundamentals, which cannot be ignored.

In the simplest terms I feel that within a balanced, stable swing the two contact points—the feet and the hands—are vital. I believe that the golf swing is built from the ground up and I will stress not only the positioning but the very active role the feet play in golf. As anything achieved by the feet and legs, the body, shoulders and arms can only be applied to the club through the hands we will also turn the spotlight on this other key area of the golfing anatomy.

My overall impression of the golf swing is of a flowing movement of continuous acceleration. My own swing tempo is fairly fast with a lot of acceleration—yours may be quicker or slower. It is unimportant as long as it has an even rhythm which accelerates the clubhead into and through the ball.

We will talk about all these aspects in much more detail later. What I would like to start with is an explanation of the causes of various types of shot. Over the years golf instruction has become so involved, and has probably had more written about it than any other sport, that most players totally overlook the beautiful simplicity of the basic concepts. Many amateur golfers, I am sure, have also lost track of what they are trying to do in a morass of words on how to do it.

The basic objectives
Golf is now such a popular sport on television and in newspapers and magazines and is played by so many people that everyone knows without giving it a second thought what the basic objects of the game are. Yet when did you last stand over a shot and actively think: 'I want to hit the ball from here to the right side of the fairway, or the left side of the green,' with a clear mental image of moving the ball from here to there. It is much more likely that you had a vague idea of where you wanted the ball to go—in the fairway or on the green—and that your mind was full of 'left arm straight, head still, cock the wrists . . .' not a clear, concise thought anywhere in sight.

What I am trying to demonstrate is that almost nobody thinks of golf in simple terms and I feel very strongly that this is where we must start. If we can strip away all the complicated clap-trap that is written and spoken about golf instruction and get down to the absolute basics of it all, I think you will agree with me that golf can be a relatively simple game. I am not suggesting that it will ever be really easy to score consistently well, but I do believe that we can all find a level of competence which can be made to work game after game, a level of consistency which will breed a more competitive spirit and bring with it a great deal more enjoyment.

If we reduce the game to the simplest terms then it becomes quite clear that the objective is to move the ball forward, in the air. Our only method of achieving this is to hit the ball with the head of the golf club. I don't intend to insult your intelligence, but quite honestly many people lose sight of these basic objectives and it is from this point on that they start to go wrong. As the clubhead hits the ball there are only three possible positions in which the clubface can be aiming—straight down the line on which you are swinging the club (square), to the left of that line (closed), or to the right of that line (open).

Contact and flight

It must be encouraging to know that whatever you may have done with your golf swing before impact, at the moment the clubhead hits the ball there can only be two possible clubface errors—open or closed. We can determine your clubface position by the flight of the ball and from this elementary beginning we can start to examine and, if necessary, to rebuild your swing from the clubface upwards. Just as the clubface is the only point of the club which makes contact with the ball, so the hands are the only part of the body which make contact with the club and it becomes immediately obvious that the open, closed or square position of the clubface can only be caused by the relative positions of the hands on the grip. In turn, the position of the hands on the grip can effect the alignment and set of the shoulders. Try a simple experiment for yourselves. Take your normal grip on the golf club and now move both hands to the right, with the right hand really under the shaft. Can you see how this automatically pushes the right shoulder down and back, pulling the left shoulder up and outwards. Now go to the other extreme, moving the hands round to the left until the right hand is completely on top of the shaft. As you move the hands you will see the right shoulder coming up and out so that it is now the same height as the left shoulder, which has moved back.

These simple experiments in your home will begin to show you that the smallest of changes in one of the fundamental positions can have far-reaching reactions throughout the swing. That is why I said at the beginning of this chapter that a wide variety of styles is quite normal and acceptable, but that certain fundamentals must be observed. And that is also why I brought a disbelieving smile to your face when I said golf was essentially a simple game.

Let us go more deeply into the mechanics of the swing in relation to your own game. Without moving from your chair you can tell me the basic

hook

slice

pull

push

The first essential factor in any plan to improve your golf is to identify your starting point. We must know how you swing the club before we can decide what improvements are necessary. This can be achieved quite simply by examining in detail your normal shot. If we know how the ball behaves when you hit it, we can trace back to the fundamentals of your swing which cause that particular reaction.

Many of you may not have a 'normal' shot which you can analyse. If you are one of those players who hits a whole range of seemingly unconnected shots, don't despair. Very often one basic fault can lead to a variety of errors. For instance, if you hit a lot of very high, weak shots, slice the ball off to the right often, yet when you aim off left to compensate, hit the ball straight left, you will be very pleased to know that all these faults and inconsistencies can be traced back to only one basic error. In the same way, the golfer who hooks the ball often, hits a lot of low shots and sometimes blasts the ball well right of the target can console himself with the knowledge that he has one basic fault, not three.

Many of the problems in golf are caused by an inability to clear away a mass of detail and get down to the root causes of the problems. The programme of analysis and understanding which forms the first part of this book is designed to show you the way in which the essentials of the golf swing are linked together and how a simple error in one department can lead to a mass of confusion.

Unfortunately a great deal of modern golf instruction is of the 'instant cure' variety, aimed specifically at business executives who can only spare ten minutes in an attempt to sort out a game which will give them lasting pleasure for the rest of their lives. Almost inevitably the majority of this type of instruction deals only with effects, not causes, plunging the golfer even deeper into the unknown. I want to strip away all the mystique and offer you a chance to understand what causes the ball to react in certain ways.

pull

hook

slice

push

The chart on this page shows quite clearly the direct relationship between the four basic shots in golf – the slice, hook, pull and push. Throughout this book we deal with swing paths and clubface positions, referring to out-to-in swing paths or open clubface positions. Let me explain here that these terms refer to an imaginary line running through the ball to the target. Thus an out-to-in swing path is one which approaches the ball from outside this line, in other words, cuts across the ball rather than hitting it squarely in the back. An open clubface position is one which points to the right of this target line.

The ideal swing path is one which approaches the ball from inside the line, moves straight along the line for a short distance before, through and after the ball and then moves inside again. The ideal clubface position is square to this line.

In addition to the ideal in-to-in swing path it is possible to swing in-to-out or out-to-in; and in addition to the perfect square clubface position the clubface can be open or closed. There are no other possibilities so we can say confidently that

there are nine possible types of golf shot, with four really common combinations. The line along which the club is swung sets the initial direction of the ball. The position of the clubface in relation to that swing line determines whether the ball flies straight or curves to the right or left.

Starting with the correct in-to-in swing path, a square clubface produces a stright shot to the target. With the clubface open the ball will start straight and fade off to the right. A closed clubface will cause a slight draw to the left.

An out-to-in swing path, with the clubface square to the swing line (not to the target line) will produce a pull, straight left of target. With an open clubface the result will be a slice, spinning off to the right. A closed clubface with this swing path will cause a pull-hook, starting left and moving further left.

With an in-to-out swing path and a square clubface (square to the swing line) the ball will fly straight, but right of the target. A closed clubface will cause a hooked shot, turning to the left, while an open clubface brings the worst result of all, a push-slice combination

with the ball starting to the right and going further away to the right.

In addition an out-to-in swing normally produces a steep, downward blow into the ball, causing high, weak shots. An in-to-out swing will usually have the clubhead approaching the ball on a very shallow angle which keeps the ball low. You can see how easy it is to hit shots towards both sides of the course with the same swing but with an inconsistent clubface position.

DISTANCE AND TRAJECTORY

The distance people hit the ball varies enormously, but I list here my normal yardages and average figures for men and women to give some indication of what you might hope to achieve. You will notice that with my medium and short irons there is a 15-yard gap between clubs, while at the upper end of the scale the gap is ten yards.

Also shown here is the type of trajectory you should achieve with various clubs. This is important, for you will only get the maximum benefit from each club when its loft is utilised correctly. If, for instance, you hit an eight-iron shot on a low five-iron trajectory you will have great trouble hitting over a bunker and stopping the ball on the green. Similarly, you will get little distance from a four-iron shot if you hit everything too high. Gradually, as we get your swing into shape and your striking becomes more consistent, you will begin to get the correct trajectory from each club.

Average club lofts are also shown here. They vary only fractionally from one manufacturer to another, although there is now a tendency to strengthen the three-wood and increase the loft of the two-wood, bringing these clubs much closer together.

irons

14

Clubs	Hale Irwin	Men	Women	Loft
1	260 yards	220	190	11
2		210	180	14
3	230-245	200	170	17
4	215-230	190	160	20
5		180	150	23
2	210	180	150	23
3	200	170	140	27
4	190	160	130	31
5	180	150	120	35
6	165	140	110	39
7	150	130	100	43
8	135	120	90	47
9	125	110	80	51
wedge	115	100	70	55
s/wedge	100	90	60	59

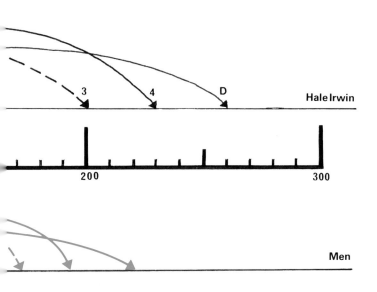

Hale Irwin

200   300

Men

woods

characteristics of your golf. You tell me how the ball behaves with your normal shot and I can tell you a lot about your golf swing. Together we can analyse the root cause of your problems. I'm not talking about the slick clichés which you hear every day on the golf course, things like 'you lifted your head,' or 'you didn't break your wrists.' These are only symptoms of the illness, not the disease itself. I know I sound like the family doctor, but this is probably the best and most graphic means of putting across my point. This is the moment where you come into your own, when you must be totally honest about your golf, because we cannot start to improve your shot-making until we have identified the exact state of your game.

The sliced shot

The right place to start has to be with the most common shot in amateur golf—the one which bends from left to right in the air—the slice. About 85 percent of the people reading this book will doubtless be nodding to themselves and saying: 'Yes, that fits my game.' But how many of you have any idea why?

A little earlier I said that if the face of the club was not in the correct square position when it hit the ball it could only be open or closed. Following our practice of tracing faults back from the clubhead, it is the open-faced position which is one of the primary causes of the slice. If everything else about the golf swing was perfect, but the face of the club was pointing to the right of the target at impact, the ball would curve off to the right as it neared the end of its flight.

You have probably noticed with your own shots that they start out fairly straight, but bend more and more in the air as they near the end of their flight. There is a very simple explanation for this. The golf ball comes off the head of the club at anything between 80–120mph, depending on whether it is hit by you, me, or Jack Nicklaus. This tremendous forward speed overrides the sidespin caused by the open clubface. But as the ball slows down towards the end of its flight the sidespin begins to take over—and away it goes, deep into the right rough.

The added penalty of slicing the ball is that the sidespin and the height of most sliced shots (we will go into the reasons for that later), add up to a loss of distance of 20 to 30 yards. On a medium length par-four hole, where a straight hitter might get home with a drive and five-iron shot, the golfer who hits the ball with the same amount of power, but who slices, will find himself perhaps 30 yards behind his partner off the tee. This will leave him two-iron distance from the green, so he will probably hit a four or five-wood second shot. The trouble is that if he slices this shot he is going to finish up 20-30 yards short and right of the green, while his partner, who hits the ball with exactly the same amount of power, can get comfortably on the green with a five-iron.

That is why the slice is such a killing shot. Overcome the problem and you will easily be hitting greens you have never got near before. What's that? You don't hit all your shots the same way? You slice your drive, yet hit a seven-iron as straight as an arrow, but 20 yards left of the green? Don't worry. it all stems from the one basic fault. Let me explain.

Just as the speed of the forward movement when the ball was hit by the driver kept the shot relatively straight for the first part of the flight, so the tremendous backspin caused by the short irons can completely override the sidespin imparted by your open clubface. The reason the ball finishes up left of the target is because you are swinging the club in that direction—a perfectly natural reaction when most of your shots bend back towards the right. This leads us very nicely into the second phase of the slice-making swing—the swing path. We have established that the ball slices to the right because contact has been made with an open clubface. We also know that the position of the clubface at impact must depend on the hands because they are the only contact with the club. As in our previous little experiment, take your normal grip on the club and then move both hands to the left, so that the right hand is virtually on top of the shaft. Now lift the head of the club off the ground and give it a few waggles. Without looking at the club take up your normal stance—and now look down and see where the clubface is pointing—way off to the right of the normal position.

This type of grip, with the hands too far to the left—as you look down on the club—is known as a weak grip. It is nothing to do with weak hands or gripping the club loosely as many people think. It designates a grip which is likely to return the clubface to the ball in an open position. We discovered earlier that this type of grip tends to pull the right shoulder upwards and outwards and pushes the left shoulder back . . . In effect this points the shoulders to the left of the target and makes it virtually impossible to swing the club along the correct path.

Correct swing path

What exactly is the correct swing path? Perhaps the easiest way to explain is to imagine that well-known golfing cliche—a golfer standing on a railway track, his feet on one line and his clubhead on the other. Let's stretch your imagination a little further by hanging a large clock pendulum from the golfer's shoulders. Then we must push the bottom of the pendulum away from him until it rests on the outside rail beside his club. I think it will become immediately obvious that the pendulum cannot swing backwards and forwards along the outside rail track. As the golfer makes his turn away from the ball in the backswing the pendulum, and his club, must come inside that track. On the downswing the club moves from inside this line, travels straight along it for a very short distance as it makes contact with the ball and then moves inside again on the follow through. In just the same way as the clubface position can only be open or closed if it is not square, so the swing line can only be too much from the inside or from outside to in if it is not correct.

In studying the normal set-up adopted by the golfer who slices we discovered that his shoulder alignment was to the left of the target and that his

Without backspin a golf ball will not fly at all. A perfectly smooth golf ball would fly only a very short distance, dipping quickly back to earth. It is not generally appreciated that the number and configuration of the dimples on a golf ball are scientifically designed to give the best results in terms of lift and stability. If the aerodynamics of the ball are not correct it will have the same effect as poor wing design on an aeroplane. The ball spins backwards with every shot, including the driver, because even the most straight faced of clubs has at least 11° of loft.

It is this backspin which allows the ball to climb on the trajectory dictated by the loft of the clubface. It also keeps the ball on line. Obviously, if the ball is in any way unbalanced, there will be a very large effect on the height and distance of its flight. Just a few dimples filled with mud will badly effect the flight of your ball and will maybe persuade you that a clean golf ball is

essential if you are to get the best results. If you have ever hit a practice ball with a cut in it you will have heard the noise the cut makes every time it spins and catches the air. Anything other than a clean, unmarked golf ball will detract from the distance you can achieve and will exaggerate any slice or hook spin you have put on the ball.

The greater the loft of the club the greater the amount of backspin imparted to the ball. This will make the ball climb more quickly into the air and will also smother the curving effect of any side spin. This is why you do not get a true picture of your golfing ability with the short irons. Any slice or hook spin will be largely overpowered by the fast

backspin. When you move to the straighter-faced clubs, perhaps to a five or four-iron, there is considerably less backspin and this allows any side spin to show its effects.

This is why many people who slice the ball to the right with the driver and long irons tend to hit the ball straight with the eight and nine-irons and the wedge. Yet so often they aim off to the left, expecting the ball to curve back to the right, that they miss their target with a pulled shot as opposed to missing with a sliced shot in the longer game. As we have seen,

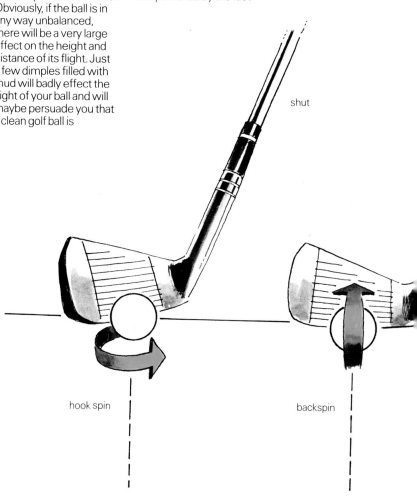

shut

hook spin

backspin

these two faults are linked by the path of the swing, which is basically aimed to the left of the target. Only the position of the clubface differs, or the loft of the shorter irons overcomes the normal effects of an open clubface.

A square clubface will hit the ball only with backspin, which is the ideal we are trying to achieve. An open clubface will spin the ball from left to right in addition to the backspin; and a closed clubface will spin the ball from right to left.

square

open

slice spin

There are only three positions in which the clubface can make contact with the ball — square, open or closed. There are no other possibilities. Add to these three positions the path of the swing on which the club approaches the ball and the vertical angle (the angle of attack) and you have the three components of the golf swing which cover the entire range open to any golfer. If you stood on the practice area for a year, you could not devise a means of hitting the golf ball that did not involve these three factors or one which introduced a new dimension to the basic golf swing.

Here we examine the ideal swing path in relation to the three clubface positions. In the backswing, the clubhead will move for a short distance straight back along the line through the ball to the target. It will then move inside that line and the downswing path will be identical, coming from inside the line, moving straight along the line until a short distance after the ball has been hit and then moving inside again. This is the in-to-in swing path.

Add a square clubface position to this swing path and it will propel the ball straight towards the target, with no side spin to drag it off line. Because the swing line and clubface positions are correct there is every reason to suppose that the angle of attack is also correct. Assuming that everything in this swing remains the same, with the exception of the clubface position, we can now look at the result when the club comes directly into the back of the ball, but the clubface is pointing to the right of the target in an open position.

Clearly the open clubface will not impart such a powerful blow to the ball as it would if it were aimed directly at the target. You can visualise the ball running down the face of the club and not collecting the full force of the impact. Because the mass of the clubhead is being swung directly at the target the ball will start in this direction, but the effects of the sidespin will soon be seen as it begins to curve off to the right. A combination of slicespin and backspin causes the ball to lose distance during its flight and also brings it quickly to a stop once it has pitched. Another factor of the open-faced shot is that the loft of the club is effectively increased as it is opened. This, in turn, will hit the ball higher.

Going to the other extreme, the correct swing path with a closed clubface will start the ball straight, but turn it left. It is a more powerful shot than the slice. The closed clubface applies more power to the ball and the hook spin helps the ball to drive forward through the air. Additionally, the loft of the club is effectively reduced by closing the face and therefore the ball will fly on a lower trajectory. The hooked shot tends to run a long way once it has pitched.

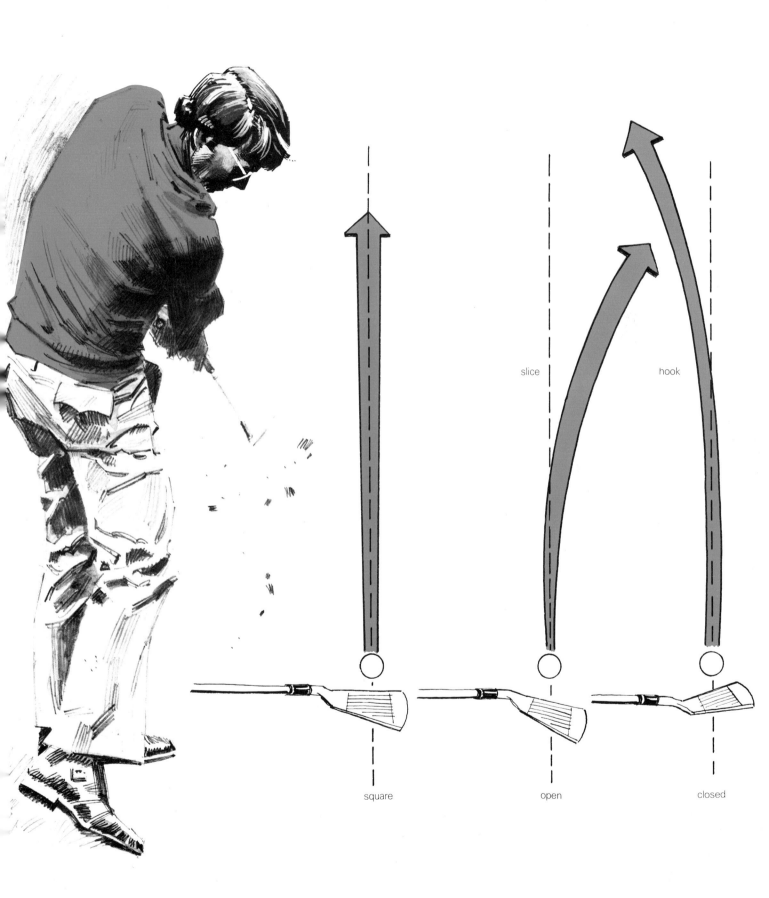

slice

hook

square

open

closed

right shoulder was too high. From this position he will almost certainly take the club away from the ball outside the rail track and it is exactly along this same path that he will return the clubhead to the ball in the downswing. So not only does he make contact with the clubface open, but with the club swinging across the ball from outside to in. It is easy to see why this glancing blow does not hit the ball as far as a properly struck shot. And there is one more factor to add frustration for the slicer. An outside-in swing line produces a fairly steep downward blow to the ball, which in turn gets it into the air very quickly, and again is a factor in reducing distance. It is because the slicer swings from out-to-in that his longer shots usually start to the left before spinning away to the right and why his short-iron shots often fly straight left. I have gone into a reasonable amount of detail in describing what causes a slice, because it is this shot which effects the largest number of players, but two general and absolute rules have emerged during the course of this discussion. The factors which govern the direction and behaviour of every golf shot are:

1) The line of the swing
2) The position of the clubface in relation to the swing line

The line of the swing sets the initial direction of the ball and the position of the clubface imparts slice or hook spin which makes the ball bend in the air.

It is the combination of these two factors which lead to the four main types of shot in golf:

1) Out-to-in swing line with clubface square to the swing line—pull
2) Out-to-in swing line with clubface open to the swing line—slice
3) In-to-out swing line with clubface square to the swing line—push
4) In-to-out swing line with clubface closed to the swing line—hook.

In addition, the out-to-in swing produces a sharp angle of attack on the ball and high-flying shots, while an exaggerated in-to-out swing produces a shallow angle of attack on the ball and low-flying shots which will often run further.

The hook and grip
We should now give a little more detailed thought to the hook shot. Because the ball bends from right to left in the air we know that contact is made with a closed clubface. We also know that a closed impact position is created by a grip which has the hands too far to the right, with the right hand often under the shaft. In turn this grip pulls the right shoulder down and back and therefore aims the shoulders to the right of the target. Almost inevitably this sets up a swing path which is too much inside the line.

What else have we learned in this examination

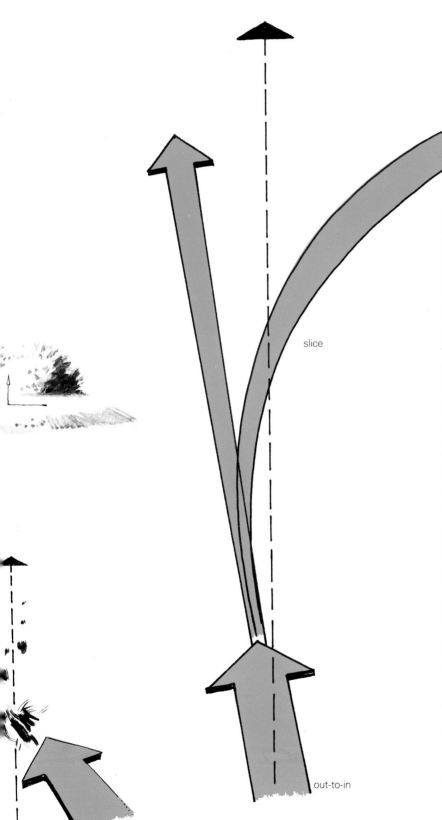

slice

out-to-in

Once we get away from the correct in-to-in swing path we start to run into trouble. With the clubhead being swung in the correct path, an open or closed clubface position will start the ball straight and will not normally bend the ball too far off in either direction. These shots will more properly be called a fade and a draw, often achieved with a fair amount of control. However, with the club being swung along an incorrect path, any deviation in the clubface position will be greatly exaggerated and this is where we really start to lose out on distance and direction.

The out-to-in swing is the most common in golf and it produces the weakest shots in the game. It starts with the clubhead being taken away from the ball slightly outside the line through the ball to the target. This usually means a steep pick up as well, for it is very difficult to keep the clubhead low on this line. Almost invariably this type of take-away leads to an identical return to the ball in the downswing. An out-to-in swing can also be caused after a correct take-away by throwing the club outside the line in the downswing by turning the shoulders into the shot instead of allowing them to follow the line of the clubhead through the ball.

As always, there will be three different effects, depending on the three possible clubface positions. With the clubface square to the line of the swing the ball will fly straight, but as the line of the swing is cutting across the line from the ball to the target it is quite obvious that the ball will finish to the left.

With an open clubface, the classic slice is achieved. The clubhead is already moving across the ball-target line and the open clubface will now hit the ball a glancing blow, lacking power and applying a great deal of sidespin. As we have already seen, the open clubface also increases the height of the shot and this is again increased because the out-to-in swing almost always produces a very steep downward angle of attack on the ball which pops it up in the air very quickly. The slice does not have anything to commend.

From time to time the person with an out-to-in swing will hit the ball with a closed clubface. As you can see this will mean the ball starting to the left of the target and going further left because of the hook spin. The trajectory will be low and the ball will continue to run a long way into trouble.

of golf's basic causes and effects? The four common golf shots fit together in pairs governed by the path of the swing. An out-to-in swing path produces a pull to the left of the target if the clubface is square and a slice bending to the right if the clubface is open. An in-to-out swing path produces a push to the right of the target if the clubface is square and a hook bending to the left if the clubface is closed.

The natural reaction

It is an unfortunate fact that the natural reactions to a slice and hook are the wrong ones. If every drive you hit tails off into the right rough then nothing is more natural than to aim further left. As we have proved to ourselves in this chapter aiming further left can only lead to a bigger slice. The reverse is equally true of the golfer who hooks and consequently aims further and further right in an effort to keep the ball in play. He merely finished up with a bigger hook.

An important point which all amateur golfers should remember, particularly the higher handicap players, is that slavish adherence to the utterances of tournament players is not a good thing. Most tournament professionals would hook the ball if they had not found some satisfactory personal method of keeping the ball reasonably straight. This is because the amount of time they devote to the game has developed strong, fast hand action which can so easily close the clubface at impact.

The majority of amateur golfers will naturally slice the ball, for the reasons I have outlined here. Very seldom does the slicer get the clubhead to the ball fast enough. He would be very foolish indeed to copy the remedies used by the tournament professional because their problems are so often at opposite ends of the golfing scale and what would be a sure cure for one would be absolute death for the other. This is an oversimplification, but I am anxious that players make corrections relevant only to their own game.

For instance, top tournament professionals are quoted so often after successful championship rounds about their suddenly improved form. They will reveal that they have been concentrating on, let us say, more leg action in the swing. For a player who naturally hooks the ball this will provide a certain safety factor, the extra leg action helping to hold the clubface square for a longer period through impact rather than allowing it to close and cause a hook. The 20-handicap player who hits the ball a glancing blow with an open clubface should not try this because his problem is exactly the opposite. While the tournament player wants to stop the clubface from closing, the handicap player will be trying to close the normally open position of his own clubface.

I have deliberately not set out any routine for practice and improvement in this chapter—that can be found in chapter four—but I would like you to understand more of the cause and effect of golf so that you have a much clearer mental picture before we attempt the modifications on your own swing.

Stick with it. I am sure it will prove worthwhile.

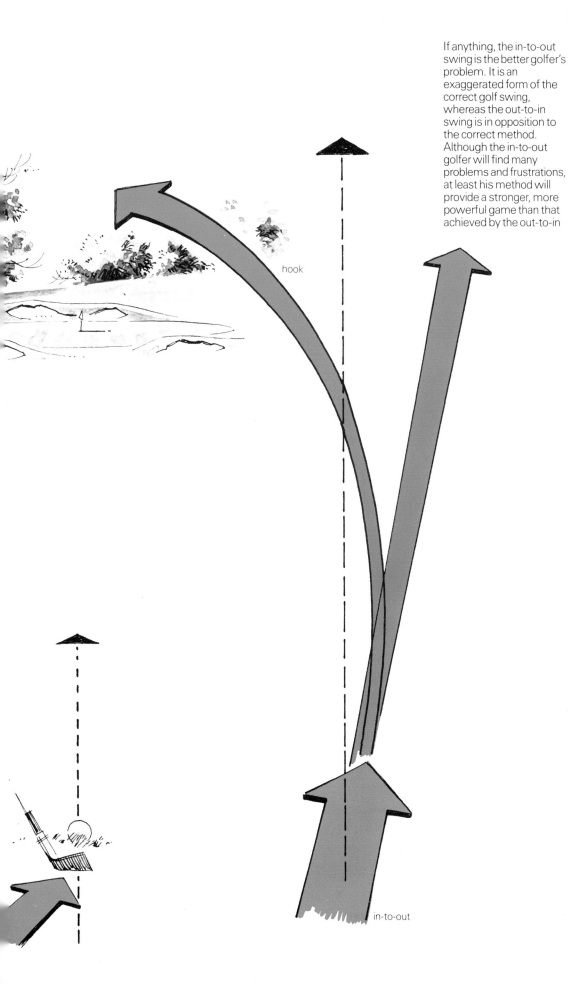

IN-TO-OUT SWING

If anything, the in-to-out swing is the better golfer's problem. It is an exaggerated form of the correct golf swing, whereas the out-to-in swing is in opposition to the correct method. Although the in-to-out golfer will find many problems and frustrations, at least his method will provide a stronger, more powerful game than that achieved by the out-to-in

The in-to-out swing is usually caused either by starting the club back too far inside the line on a very low path, or by dropping the club down and back at the top of the backswing, thus attacking the ball from the inside.

This type of swing path with a clubface which is square to that swing line will hit the ball straight to the right of the target. This is known as a push shot and is the type of shot often produced by good players under pressure because they will not allow their normal free release through the ball, and try to steer the ball to the target.

Although an open clubface is not a normal occurrence with this type of swing, it does sometimes happen. With this you can achieve one of the worst shots in the game, the ball which starts out to the right and slices away further right all the time.

However, the more normal shot will be caused by a combination of in-to-out swing and closed clubface. This will produce a hooked shot which will start out along the line of the swing, to the right of the target, but bend back to the left. Because the clubface is closed at impact and the effective loft of the club therefore reduced, the ball will fly lower than normal. The combination of hook spin and low trajectory means that it will run a long way. Under control, it can be a most effective shot, gaining a great deal of distance. Out of control it can get you into more trouble than almost any other shot in the game.

hook

in-to-out

How do you shape up?

The most important element of the stance is to achieve a feeling of stability and balance because everything you do before beginning to swing causes a reaction throughout your golf. You must have a feeling of being well set, yet poised for action.

Physical shape and size have a direct bearing on the way a golfer builds his swing. It is important to harness what nature has given you rather than fighting against it. The most obvious factor is the plane of the swing and it is extremely helpful to watch in action a professional whose build resembles your own.

Now that we have completed a mental analysis of your swing we are ready to make a move, but only as far as your nearest full-length mirror. There are still several important points to be clarified before we get to the golf course. These lessons relate to the vital aspects of the swing set-up, to alignment and to swing plane. What you must realise is that what happens in the set-up can make or break your golf. Everything you do before you begin to swing causes reactions throughout your golf.

I have already mentioned briefly that in my opinion the feet play an important part throughout the swing. We aren't going to be swinging the club just yet, but the correct stance also starts with the feet.

The right stance

First we must consider how far apart the feet should be and the positions they take up in relation to each other. We are discussing full shots at the moment, we will get down to the shorter clubs later, and the most important thing to achieve in your stance is a feeling of stability and balance. A good guide is to have the feet the same width apart as the shoulders. Now whether this means the inside or the outside of the feet at shoulder width is of no great importance and is a matter of personal choice and comfort. Stability and balance are the essential factors. Weight should most definitely be on the insides of the feet—and, in fact, it remains there until the start of the downswing. If you can feel that your bodyweight is firmly planted on the inside of each foot, just in front of the heels, then you have probably got the ideal starting point. You must have a feeling of being well set, yet poised for

action. This cannot be the case if you are putting too much weight on one foot or if the weight is too close to the toes or heels so that you are in danger of falling forwards or backwards. It may not seem a very important point—and judging from some of the address positions I see it certainly is not with many amateurs—but the angle at which the feet are set has repercussions throughout the swing. One of the most essential elements in the backswing is a build up of power around a firm position. This can best be accomplished by having the right foot turned out to the right at a very slight angle—20-30 degrees maximum so that the backswing turn is around a line drawn upwards from the inside of the right heel.

Try a few backswing turns yourself, first with the right foot turned out 45 degrees or more and then at only 20 degrees. You will feel the difference in the tension of the legs, hips, and shoulders and might feel that this restricts your backswing. If it does it will almost certainly prove beneficial because you will be achieving the same amount of wind-up with an essentially shorter and more controlled action. One of the dangers of a slack right foot position is that you can turn too far too easily and this can lead to sloppiness in the downswing.

A few problems

The other problem with an outward pointing right foot is that it is an open invitation to sway to the right off the ball in the backswing. Point the right foot forwards and get the feeling that the right knee is pointing in towards the ball and you willl have a really solid foundation for your swing.

As far as the left foot is concerned, this is the

one you can point more towards the target because the freedom of turn you want to guard against in the backswing is the very action you must promote through impact. The feet are also important for the reason that the positioning of the ball is in relation to the stance. Ideally the ball should be played directly in front of the left heel, certainly for all long shots. We can discuss the possibilities of slight variations for shorter shots at the appropriate time.

What have the knees been up to while all this has been going on at ground level? I mentioned just now that the right knee should be kinked in slightly towards the ball. This should be matched by the left knee. If you really do have your weight evenly split between the insides of both feet this will be virtually automatic. But, of course, the knees also have to flex and as the entire body posture is vitally affected by the position of the knees you can begin to understand that they take on an importance you may not have imagined.

Let me explain the reason for flexing the knees and perhaps it will fall into place for you more easily. Although we should all retain as much body height as we can reasonably manage throughout the swing, because this leads to a wider swing arc, more clubhead speed and greater distance, you can see it would be absolutely impossible to achieve any sort of smooth swing action with completely stiff legs. Try a few swings and see what I mean. And would you attempt to jump across a stream from a straight-legged position? Of course you wouldn't.

The knees must be flexed to allow a proper turn away from the ball in the backswing and the full release of power through the ball. It is only with the flexibility given by the knees that we can hope to achieve any rhythm and balance in the swing. So let's get it right.

Mirror, mirror
Stand in front of your mirror as if you were hitting towards a green on the other side of the glass. Take your normal grip on the club, but keep your legs and body completely straight. Watch yourself in the mirror over your left shoulder and tilt at the waist until your upper body and head have moved forward just a few degrees and the head of your club is two or three inches off the floor. Maintaining this position, flex your knees just enough to get the clubhead on the floor. Take a good look at yourself in this position because it is from here that you will achieve your best results.

Go through the routine a few times until you get the feel imprinted on your mind. It will probably feel very strange because the chances are that you have either been bending too far from the waist and not flexing the knees enough, or flexing the knees too much and keeping your back too straight. To help you find the correct position we have included drawings of several top professionals of varying builds so that you can find someone approximately your own shape and size. You will notice that a vertical line through the centre of the head leads down through the knees to the feet.

You can see how interrelated all these aspects of the golf game are, because in setting out to

Every golfer can benefit from watching a professional golfer who resembles him in size and build. It is much easier to model your swing on that of someone your own shape than to try and adapt. This does not mean copying everything that your look-alike pro might do, but certainly in terms of set-up and swing plane you can pay close attention.

Ben Hogan had the best way of explaining swing plane. He asked golfers to imagine that as they addressed the ball they had their heads through a hole in an enormous sheet of glass which rested on their shoulders and touched the ground just beyond the ball. The piece of glass was the swing plane and from half-way up the backswing into the follow through the arms and club should swing just below the glass's surface.

The vital thing to realise is that the plane on which you swing the club is dictated largely by your size. In general terms tall golfers swing the club on a more upright plane than shorter players. Take Tom Weiskopf and Gary Player, two world-class players who are just about as far apart as you can get in terms of physical size. Tom stands quite close to the ball and swings the club on an upright plane. His height assures him of a large swing arc — the curve described by the head of the club during the swing. It is the size of the swing arc which allows the clubhead to be swung as fast as possible on the downswing and leads to greater distance.

Obviously, if Gary Player swung the club on the same plane as Tom Weiskopf the arc followed by his clubhead would be far shorter. In fact Gary adopts, quite naturally, a flatter swing plane. This means that he swings the club more round his body than the up-and-down action used by Tom Weiskopf. This enables the smaller golfer to increase his swing arc to the maximum.

It is a mistake to fight nature's gifts. Do what the great golfers do — adapt your techniques to suit your own particular build. The best way to achieve that is to copy someone your own size.

explain the importance of knee flex we have quite naturally moved on to cover the complete body posture in profile—in other words, in looking at the set up from the line through the ball to the target. Now we must consider the matter from another angle. This time face directly into the mirror and go through your posture routine. This is now the position from which you hope to hit the ball down the centre of the fairway. What are your chances?

Arm and shoulder

The keys to the set-up from this angle are the left arm and the right shoulder. If these are correct it is very difficult for the rest of the body to be out of position. From the left shoulder, down the arm, through the hand and down the club shaft to the ball should be fairly close to a straight line. That does not mean it should be rigid or that the grip should be like a clamp on the club. A reasonably firm grip with the last three fingers of the left hand will aid control. What you should avoid is the hands behind the clubhead so that there is a distinct angle in the arm-club line, for this tends to cause a wristy, imprecise take-away from the ball. This vital relationship between the left arm and the club sets the radius for the whole swing and forms the key part of the movement necessary to return the club to the ball repetitively and consistently. 'Keep the left arm straight' is one of the oldest instructional cliches in the game, and a very valid one—yet the sheer rigidity of the phrase has probably caused as many problems as it has cured. Throughout the backswing the left arm should be as straight as you can keep it without ever being stiff and without ever inducing tension in the wrist or the shoulder. It is the means of controlling the arc of the swing and if you can have the mental image of keeping the grip of the club at the same distance from the left shoulder right through the backswing, rather than of holding the left arm straight, you will probably achieve your objective more easily.

If you adopt your set-up position by taking your left hand grip on the club and placing the clubhead behind the ball you can then complete the all-important triangle between the hands, arms and shoulders by reaching down and under to place your right hand on the grip, adjusting the final position of the hands into your correct grip. We will go into this later as grip adjustments come under the rebuilding programme suggested by your complete swing analysis.

Weak grip

The reason I ask you to reach down and under in placing your right hand on the club is that this will ensure the right shoulder stays lower than the left. So often golfers reach out and around for the right hand grip and this leaves them with the weak grip we discussed in the first chapter and leads to the shoulders being virtually level. From this address position it is extremely difficult to take the club away from the ball back along the target line and then inside. It almost invariably causes an outside take-away and the slicer's out-to-in swing steeply across the ball.

There are certain restrictions nature places

We discovered in the first chapter the importance of the three clubface positions, square, open or closed, and saw what dramatic effects these differing positions has on the flight of the ball. The way you grip the club is going to have the greatest single affect on the position of the clubface, but it is not generally realised to what extent the grip can also effect the entire set-up position.

Take the two extreme cases shown here – the very weak and the exceptionally strong grips. These terms do not refer to the power or tension of the grip, but to the positioning of the hands. A weak grip is one which places the hands too far to the left as the golfer looks down on the club.

The right hand will appear to be on top of the shaft. This will lead to an open clubface position and a sliced shot. A strong grip moves the hands too far to the right, with the right hand creeping under the shaft. This creates a closed clubface position

and leads to hooked shots.

Now look at the other effects. With the right hand on top of the shaft in a weak grip the right shoulder has moved up and forward. This opens the shoulder line more than is necessary. Because the right shoulder starts in a high position, there will be a steep pickup of the clubhead in the backswing and almost certainly the club will be taken outside the line. This is the classic set-up position for the golfer who slices the ball.

At the other end of the scale, the very strong grip, with the right hand under the shaft, pulls the right shoulder too low and moves it backwards away from the ball. This has the opposite effect to the weak grip, closing the shoulder line, making it point to the right of the target. The very low position of the right shoulder will cause a take-away of the club from the ball on a very inside line, bringing about the in-to-out swing. This is the prime example of a hooking set-up.

The only contact we have with the club, and therefore the only means of controlling the ball, comes through the hands. Very few golfers realise the far-reaching effects of an incorrect grip or the effects that can be achieved throughout the swing with a very small change of hand positions.

upon us which have a great effect on the way we swing a golf club. In general terms shorter people swing the club on a flat plane and taller golfers have a more upright action. I feel that it can help everyone to find a professional golfer, or top amateur, who is built along similar lines to themselves so that they have a model on which to base their own action. This does not mean copying everything their look-alike pro might do, but the overall set-up and swing impression can be very important.

Size wise

Take Gary Player and Tom Weiskopf as two examples of first-class world players at opposite ends of the size scales. Gary is 5ft 8ins and weighs 158lbs, while Tom measures a comfortable 6ft 3ins. Gary stands further away from the ball and this leads to a flatter swing, more round the body, while Tom stands much closer to the ball and therefore swings on a more upright plane, more up and down than round.

Try this experiment yourself. Take any club and address the ball normally. Now flex your knees more and more, reducing your height by six inches, but retaining the rest of your set-up position, and see how the head of the club slides along the ground away from you. This shows clearly why shorter people must position the ball further away—in general it is not necessary for them to have shorter clubs (see the chapter on equipment). It is a mistake to fight these natural tendencies. Accept them for what they are and make them work to your advantage.

How do you find the correct distance to stand from the ball? It is not easy to give hard and fast rules, but it is something every player can work out for himself.

Take your normal grip and stance and pull the head of the club closer and closer towards your feet and you will see that your arms will bend and the heel of the club will come off the ground. Push the clubhead away and the toe of the club will stick up in the air. The mid-way position, with the sole of the club flat on the ground, is your own ideal position. We will deal later with equipment and how to find the club which suits you best. However, it you feel that your own clubs are hurting your game you should have them checked out by a pro. Don't build your game around an ill-fitting set of clubs.

The basic plane of the swing is on a line drawn through the shoulders to the clubhead. The best illustration of the plane of the swing that I have ever heard came from the great Ben Hogan. He would ask golfers to imagine that their head was sticking through a hole in a large sheet of glass which was resting on their shoulders, with the edge touching the ground just beyond the ball. The glass was the perfect swing plane and the hands, arms and club had to parallel that line throughout the swing. In fact, because the hands quite naturally fall below this line at address, it is midway through the backswing before the left arm and club shaft really start to parallel the sheet of glass that closely. Hogan felt, and I agree completely, that the hands should never crash through the glass,

The golf swing is a delicate balance of rhythm and power and there is no way this can be fully achieved if your set-up position incorporates bad posture. The ideal golfing posture should allow the weight to be evenly spread between the insides of both feet, with the knees sufficiently flexed to enable a smooth turn away from the ball in the backswing and a flowing movement through the ball at impact. The body should be angled just enough to allow a free movement of the arms through the ball, while still retaining as much body height as possible.

There are two incorrect positions which I see repeated most often. There is the straight back, with almost no bend at the waist but knees flexed too much to compensate. The other extreme keeps the knees straight and rigid but the body bends over far too much from the waist.

Remembering that we wish to retain as much body height as we can to increase the swing arc and help develop clubhead speed and power, the knees must be flexed just enough to allow a fluid movement in the backswing and through swing. Perhaps the best way to achieve your correct posture is to study a professional of your own build again, watching carefully as he sets up to the ball and then try to emulate this position in front of your mirror at home.

Go through this exercise in front of your mirror. Stand upright with the legs straight, and take your normal grip on the club. Now bend over at the waist just a few degrees until your arms are hanging just clear of the body. This should put the head of the club two or three inches above the floor. Now flex your knees until the clubhead rests on the floor. This should put you in much the same position as the pro you have been studying. When viewed from the front, your set-up should show a virtually straight line from the left shoulder, through the left arm and club shaft to the ball. The right shoulder will be lower than the left and the weight will, if anything, be slightly more biased towards the left side.

Get used to this position by repeating it several times in front of the mirror so that you can fall into place quite naturally on the first tee, when there will be no mirror to help you get set.

All the elements of sound sand play – eye on the ball, firm stance and excellent shoulder, arm and wrist action as the ball rises right out of the trap. Take special note of the wrist and the position of the club head.

should never be above the natural swing plane, for this leads to all types of errors, most likely a downswing outside the normal line—which leads us straight back into slicer's territory again.

The last item we can cross off our checklist by using the mirror technique is alignment. Imagining that the target is the other side of the mirror we can see if we are squared up correctly with feet, knees and hips parallel to the target line. The shoulders should fall into a natural and comfortable position slightly left of the target. Alignment is vital in two respects. If the line through your feet is pointing to the right of the target and the line through your shoulders to the left, one will be fighting the other throughout the swing. Getting the active parts of the body working in unison can only be achieved if they start in the correct relationship to each other. It is no good hitting the best shot in the world if you have lined yourself up 20 yards right of the green and the majority of people do aim too far right. Using our mirror technique we can check both at once.

Lining up

It is very obvious if the feet, knees, hips or shoulders are positioned out of line, but not so easy to assess how you are lining up on target. Very many people look across their left shoulder at the green but in reality this causes a very closed shoulder position pointing well to the right of where you intend the ball to go. The trick is to look along the front of your shoulder and make that line aim at the left edge of your target, maintaining the stance alignment reasonably direct at target. A good tip is to hold a club against your shoulders so that the shaft forms an extension of your shoulder line. You may have the impression of aiming left, but when the club shaft points straight at itself in the mirror you know you have got it absolutely square. A slightly open shoulder line, with the end of the shaft pointing slightly left, would be quite correct.

I want to stress the importance of correct set-up and alignment, for once you have started the swing you do not want to be making adjustments —it is virtually impossible and can lead to a mass of errors. Try to get everything right before you start the swing. This should not prove too difficult as the ball is stationary and you have only to set yourself in the correct position in relation to the ball. Yet, as we have seen, the smallest error in the set-up can cause a chain reaction which will have serious repercussions throughout the swing. With a relatively small amount of study and application every golfer should be capable of achieving the correct set-up, the vital starting point without which a proper swing cannot take place.

Alignment is another factor which takes place before the swing starts—and here again there is really no excuse for not getting it right. Correct alignment of the club and body allows a full, free swing through the ball and ensures that when you hit your best shot it goes where you intended. The factors over which the golfer has complete control, those which take place before the club is swung, play a vital part in the golf swing and should not be ignored.

LINING UP

One of the most basic aspects of golf and one which causes untold problems is alignment. Even tournament professionals go through phases where they find it difficult to line up properly on target.

Here again you can achieve a great deal by using a mirror to check your own position. What you are trying to achieve is a position in which your feet are parallel to the line running through the ball to the target, the hips and shoulders pointing fractionally left of that line. This is the ideal set-up, allowing you to swing the club on the correct in-to-in path, with the slight opening of the hip and shoulder position encouraging a full hit through the ball towards the target. If the hip and shoulder alignment were to the right of the target, in a closed position, this would block the left side and prevent the arms and club swinging through directly on line.

Address a ball as if you were going to hit it at the mirror, as if the green was on the far side of the looking glass. Your right foot should be directly behind the left, on the same line, but you should just be able to see your right shoulder in front of the left. To help spot this you can hold a club across the front of your shoulders. This gives a better indication of the line along which they are aimed.

A great many people aim incorrectly over their left shoulder, getting themselves into a position where they are pointing well right of the

target. If you are one of these people, your right shoulder will be completely hidden as you study your position in the mirror. You can also check the effects of a strong and weak grip while in this position. With the right hand on top of the shaft

you will see that the right shoulder is pulled well forward into view. With the right hand underneath the shaft the right shoulder disappears from view behind the left.

Continue to work on your set-up and alignment on the practice area, placing two clubs on the ground pointing at the target – one to line up your feet and the other on the far side of the ball so that you have an easy

reference line with which to square up the clubface. When you have lined up correctly with the clubs on the ground, look over your left shoulder and note its position in relation to your target. This is what you are trying to achieve on every shot.

THREE BASIC GRIPS

Without doubt the most popular grip in the history of the game is the one pioneered by that famous British professional, Harry Vardon. Known universally as the Vardon grip it overlaps the little finger of the right hand on the first finger of the left hand. It is an ideal way of getting the hands close together without tension.

For those who like to have a more definite link between the hands, the interlock may be the answer. It entwines the little finger of the right hand with the first finger of the left.

The third choice is for those who have small hands or who like to get as solid a grip on the club as they can. This is the two-handed or baseball grip. As the name implies, both hands are fully on the club shaft, with no overlap or interlock of the fingers.

The other important thing to remember is the grip pressure. Obviously you need to hold the club firmly enough to be able to swing it fast without fear of losing control. Yet at the same time you must not try to choke it to death. Any undue tension in the hands and wrists will affect the arms and the rest of the swing. The grip should be light yet firm at address.

overlap Vardon

interlock

baseball (two handed)

Swing thoughts and style

The ability to watch and imitate is critical. It is important to mix fact with feel if we are ever to fully appreciate the finer points of the game—and this is where mental images are so valuable.

In an attempt to match the proven facts of golf swing technique with the actual feel of the club during the swing it can be very helpful to work with a series of mental images. The right set of mental pictures can last you a golfing lifetime.

Before we set foot on the practice tee, I would like to give you my overall impressions of the golf swing so that we will be fully armed with all the necessary information by the time we start to pull your game into better shape.

Young children have the best chance to learn easily. Their ability to watch and imitate is immense. I believe it is said that we learn as much in the first seven years of our lives as we do in the remainder and certainly if you have children who are interested in sport you should get them a few professional golf lessons while they are young. They will pick the game up very easily and it will stay with them for ever. So it is very important that they learn correctly—mistakes learned at this stage will be ingrained for life. Assuming that your best learning years are already behind you I believe it is important with a game like golf to mix fact with feel if we are ever fully to appreciate the finer points of the sport—and this is where mental images can be so valuable.

Mental image

My father gave me the best mental picture of the golf swing I have ever heard. He always felt it was like using an old-fashioned scythe. I used to cut the grass at home with one when I was a boy and believe me that was an implement you just couldn't rush. It had a long handle which needed both hands, and a large, heavy head. If you didn't develop a steady rhythm you were in great danger of chopping off a leg—almost certainly your own.

It was such a long, difficult tool to use that you had to take up a well-balanced footing and move it very easily and rhythmically with a backswing and through swing. Because the golf club is so light and easy to move by comparison, there is so often a tendency to rush the swing, many people thrashing into the downswing before the backswing has been completed. In no way was that possible with a scythe. I have always carried that image in my mind on the golf course and have added to it over the years because not only is golf a game of smooth rhythm, but also an action of continuous acceleration.

As far as I am concerned the golf swing is from the top of the backswing to the end of the follow through. The backswing is part of the overall swing but, in fact, I prefer to think that the club is placed at the top of the backswing, almost unconsciously. So the acceleration I refer to is from the top, through impact, tailing off to the finish. No golf shot can be hit properly unless the downswing accelerates the clubhead into the ball. This applies not only to full shots with the big clubs like the driver, but to the smallest chip shots and even to putts. The whole basis of the golf swing is a motion of continuous acceleration. In order to make yourself generate the maximum acceleration through the impact area it is sometimes a good tip to think of requiring the greatest clubhead speed a foot beyond the ball. This is not really the case, but it does have the effect of getting much greater clubhead speed when the ball is struck.

Diagnosis and cure

The worst aspect of a decelerating golf swing is that it leads to inconsistent contact with the ball. This means that any swing faults you have are made worse, yet at the same time you do not get a

SCYTHE SWING BUILDS RHYTHM

It is essential that the transition from backswing to forward swing should be smooth and unhurried, with the distinct feeling that the backswing is complete before the rhythmic acceleration starts. The tendency to rush from backswing to downswing often destroys the golfers rhythm.

Firmly implant in your mind the image of swinging a scythe while you are handling a golf club and try to feel in particular the completion of an evenly paced backswing and a smooth transition into an accelerating downswing. The extra weight of swinging two or three clubs together can often help to obtain this feel. It is much more difficult to rush things with a heavier weight. For these reasons it can be quite helpful to swing a long-handled brush. The important thing is to implant in your mind and your muscles the correct impression of an evenly-paced backswing and an accelerating downswing, allowing the natural completion of the backswing before starting down.

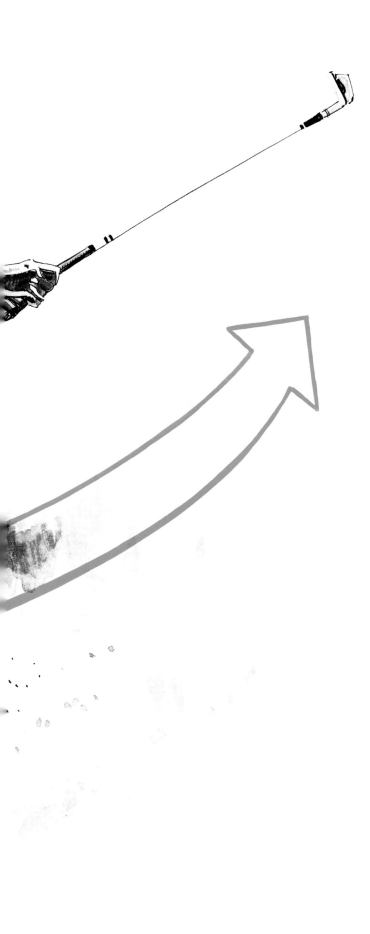

consistent reaction between the club and the ball
and therefore the behaviour of the ball and the
consequent diagnosis of the basic faults is much
harder to establish.

Try a few eight-iron shots with a half-swing, but
making a crisp movement with the clubhead
through the ball. You will be amazed at how well
and how far the ball will fly. Get used to
accelerating the clubhead in small shots and
gradually you will build it into your entire game.

As I mentioned in the opening pages of the
book I am a great believer in the fact that we hit the
ball with the clubhead and we hold the club in the
hands—therefore the hands are a key point in
the golf game. I also mentioned that our only
point of contact with the ground was through our
feet and I therefore nominated the feet as the
second key point. Just imagine trying to swing a
golf club in the middle of an ice rink and you will
begin to understand what I mean.

Vital feet

The feet serve two vital functions and I always
feel that the swing literally starts from the feet and
works up the body. Take the case of trying to play
golf on ice and see exactly how much you would
lose. As you turned the hips and shoulders away
from the ball in the backswing there would be no
build up of power in the muscles, no resistance
from the feet to coil what we might call the
backspring, because the feet would slide to the
position of least resistance.

You have probably seen people from your own
club achieving just such a negative position on the
first tee—not standing on a block of ice, but
getting the same results by allowing the left foot to
come right up on to the toe at the top of the
backswing and thus releasing any muscle coil
which might have been built up. You can feel this
quite clearly by swinging into your normal
backswing position and then suddenly lifting the
left heel clear of the ground. Virtually all the
muscle tension that can be felt in the thighs, hips
and shoulders will disappear. There is no harm in
allowing the left heel to lift slightly off the ground,
but it should remain a controlling factor in the
backswing.

The equally important second function of the
feet is to guide the weight shift which occurs in the
downswing and which thus controls much of the
rhythm and balance of the entire swing. A great
deal has been said and written about starting the
downswing with a movement towards the ball of
the right knee or of leading with a slide of the left
hip etc., etc., but all of these ideas will be much less
effective if you have a flat-footed action. Any
attempt to move the right knee or slide the left hip
must have an effect on the feet—and if the feet
don't respond, nothing much will happen at all.

I just happen to believe it is much more logical
to go straight to the heart of the matter, to the
point beyond which this effect cannot go any
further—to the feet. Study any good golf swing in
the modern game and you will see quite clearly
that at the top of the backswing the whole
movement has pivoted around the right leg. In
the downswing the weight and momentum move
across to the left leg. Look again at the swing and

FEET ANCHOR THE SWING

loss of control (detail foot)

For all the benefit they get from their footwork, many golfers would be just as effective if they were standing on a block of ice. Throughout the swing the feet should retain a firm, controlled relationship with the ground. A simple experiment will show you one of the main reasons.

Take as full a backswing as you can manage while keeping the left heel firmly on the ground. You will feel muscle pressure in the legs, hips and shoulders as your body coils into the backswing. This is the build-up of muscle power which will release the clubhead into the ball at impact.

Now see how quickly this muscle tension disappears if you lift your left heel well clear of the ground – and this is merely an exaggerated form of the poor footwork to be found so often among handicap golfers. If the feet do not work positively and correctly, there will be a tremendous loss of the latent power necessary to move the clubhead fast into the ball.

In addition there will be a great loss of control. Any excessive lift of the left heel in the backswing will also encourage a fuller turn, because there is little resistance, and the very real chance of swaying to the right, behind the ball. Swaying away from the ball in the backswing requires an equal sway back towards the ball in the downswing

The backswing should take place round a flexed, but firm right leg, the major part of the body weight never moving further back than the inside of the right foot. In the majority of shots it should be sufficient to allow the left foot to roll to the right in order to achieve a good backswing turn, although on long shots I lift the left heel slightly while still keeping a firm position.

I would much rather see golfers with shorter swings where the body and the club are under control than bigger turns achieved at the expense of sloppy foot action.

now study the feet in detail. You will notice that at address the weight is evenly balanced between the insides of both feet. At the top of the backswing 60 percent of the weight is on the inside of the right foot and as the downswing starts the weight shifts to the outside of the left foot, which eventually rolls over on to its side towards the completion of the swing. Having seen the action of the feet in a good swing, can we reverse the process and, by making the feet behave this way, get the rest of the swing to fall into place behind? I believe we can.

On the practice tee you can say to yourself 'inside right—outside left' as you swing the club backwards and forwards. You will soon find that building your swing from the feet really does work. By concentrating the shift of weight in the feet it is very difficult for any other part of the body to get out of position and out of rhythm. Equally, if the balance of the feet is correct the balance of the swing will follow more easily. If you take several practice swings while standing on the same spot you can check your footprints to see if you are getting through correctly on to the left foot. You will clearly see a heavy indentation where the right foot was placed and a deeper one down the outside edge of the left imprint but without a heavy emphasis towards the toe or heel.

I regard the backswing as important only for the reason that it puts the club in the right position to start the business part of the swing and there are two factors which govern correct club position at the top of the backswing—height and line.

Ideally the shaft of the club should be no further back than horizontal at the top of the swing and should be pointing directly parallel to the target line. Successful golf can be played without achieving these ideals, but go beyond them and you are courting trouble. Failure to get the club back as far as horizontal is by no means drastic and is certainly a great deal better than allowing it to go too far, for this inevitably leads to lack of control.

Keeping control

If you have trouble achieving the ideal, make sure you come out on the right side. In other words, stopping short of the perfect position will possibly prevent you from achieving perfection, but no corrections will be necessary to attain a reasonable performance. Anytime you have to correct a mistake to achieve the proper result, you multiply your chances of hitting a poor shot.

The object of getting the club back to a horizontal position is to achieve maximum distance without losing control. The length of the arc of the swing helps generate clubhead speed and therefore distance—the further and wider the clubhead travels the better, within reasonable limits of control. But I would rather see the hands reach a reasonably high position with the club failing to get as far as the horizontal position than a low hand position losing control of the club and allowing it to fall below horizontal.

Two prime reasons for loss of control at the top of the backswing are too big a turn away from the ball, which we have seen is a result of poor foot action, and failure to retain a proper grip on the

ACCELERATION

Acceleration of the clubhead is a vital factor in every golf shot from a five-foot putt to a 250-yard drive. Acceleration is involved with more than just the provision of power – you don't need too much of that for a five-foot putt. Acceleration, within the framework of your swing tempo, provides a consistent method of making contact with the ball – a repeating pattern which is essential to achieve any real level of performance.

With a known swing tempo – that which is best suited to you as an individual golfer – and a given length of backswing, an acceleration of the clubhead into the impact area will lead to a consistent contact with the ball. It is comparatively easy to accelerate the clubhead on a repeating basis; it is impossible – and undesirable – to decelerate into the ball by the same amount each time you swing.

In addition to the obvious loss of power which a decelerating swing will produce, the lack of a consistent strike will make judgement of distance particularly difficult. This lack of a consistent reaction between the club and the ball can lead to a variety of miss-hit shots and makes the diagnosis of basic swing faults that much more difficult.

I personally regard the golf swing, that is from the top of the backswing through impact, as a movement of continuous acceleration. I feel that within my own swing tempo I accelerate the clubhead a great deal. Yet this is an area where fact and feel contradict each other. In reality, if the clubhead is travelling at its maximum speed as it makes contact with the ball, acceleration must have stopped just before impact. Think of it logically. Acceleration means an increase in the existing speed. However, the feeling you should have when hitting the ball is that the clubhead is still accelerating at the moment of impact.

It is often helpful to deliberately feel that the fastest point of the swing is just beyond impact. Of course, this is not scientifically correct, but it does help to ensure that there is no tendency to slow down the clubhead before the ball. It also helps to keep the clubhead firmly on line well through the strike area – a very useful side-effect which can only help improve the squareness of the clubface on impact.

Correct acceleration can only be achieved if the position of the body and of the club is correct at the top of the backswing. I believe that the backswing sets up the power coil in the body and places the club in the right position in terms of direction and length of swing. It is the release of the latent power built up in the backswing, along the proper swing path, which leads not only to powerful, but accurate shot-making.

This action is repeated in even the shortest of chip shots and putts. The clubhead should always accelerate to ensure firm contact with the ball.

FOOTWORK

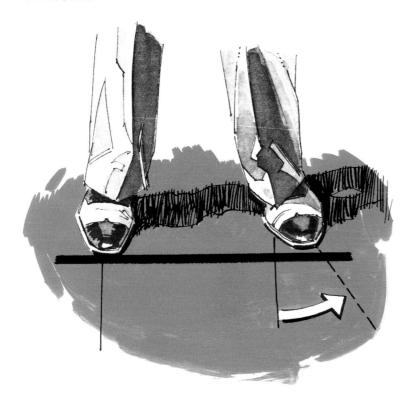

The part played by the feet in the golf swing is regarded by many people as passive – a mere following of the lead given by the hips, legs and knees. In fact a very large proportion of golfers give no thought to the feet at all. I firmly believe that the feet play an active role in the golf swing. Rather than the feet reacting to the movements of the body and legs.

First-class golf swings have a common factor of good footwork. They cannot be built on an immovable, flat-footed base, nor one on which the feet do not retain a controlling contact with the ground.

Rather than starting the downswing with a slide of the hips to the left or by moving the right knee in behind the ball, two of the more common theories, I believe the downswing starts with a transfer of weight from the inside of the right foot to the outside of the left foot.

A close study of foot action shows that at address the ideal position has the body weight evenly divided between the feet, concentrated at a point towards the front and on the inside of each foot. During the backswing turn about 60 percent of the weight moves to the inside of the right foot. Care should be taken to avoid weight moving to the outside of the right foot as this will encourage a sway away from the ball.

At the start of the downswing the weight shifts across to the outside of the left foot. By using the feet as a checkpoint for weight transfer, I believe you will find it easier to establish the correct rhythm and balance throughout your swing. You will find the right knee coming in behind the ball and the hips sliding to the left, but because we are starting from the ground and working up they will fall more properly into place within the framework of the overall swing.

You can check your weight transfer by hitting several shots on the practice area without moving your feet and then looking at the indentations you have made in the turf. The deepest points should be down the left side of both the right and left foot imprints.

Another way in which the feet can help the overall swing is by adjusting the angles of the feet at address. By having the right foot pointing almost straight forward you will find it easier to keep the weight on the inside of this foot in the backswing. In turn this will prevent a sway away from the ball. By turning the left foot out slightly at address, allowing it to point more towards the target, you will encourage a full and easy transfer of weight to the left in the downswing.

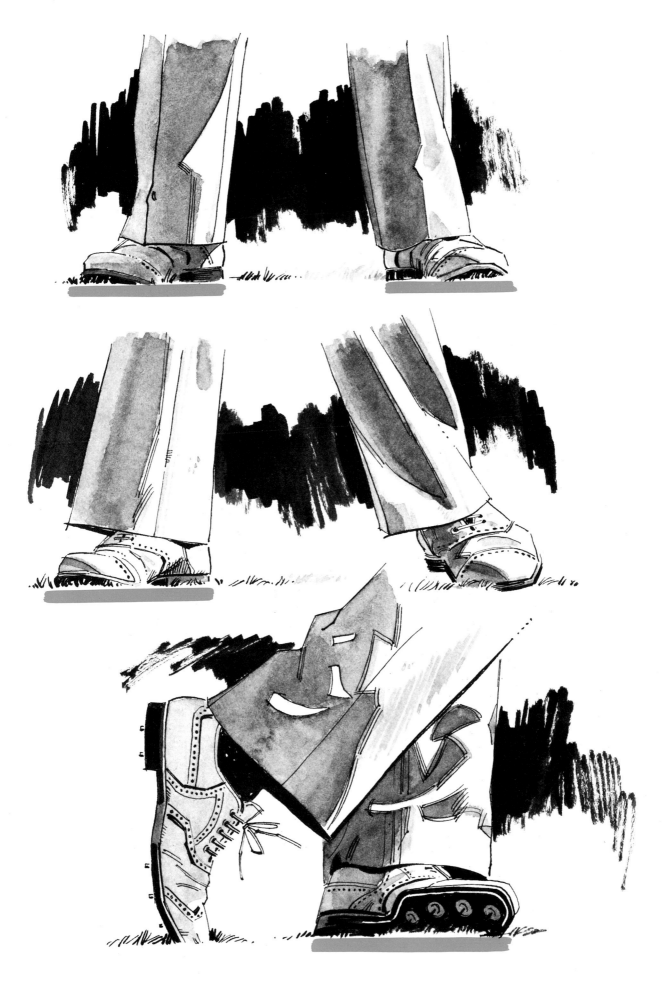

BACKLIFT LENGTH

The backswing is designed to coil latent power into the body which is released through a fast-moving clubhead into the ball. This release can only be effectively achieved if the backswing also sets the club in the right position.

In attempting a full backswing turn a great many problems can be caused. We have already seen how the left heel can be dragged well off the ground, leading to a loss of coiling power and encouraging a sway to the right. Here we are concerned with the arms and hands.

I have never advocated a stiff left arm because this brings tension into the golf swing. The left arm is the key link between the body and the club and its purpose, without stiffness or tension is to maintain, as far as possible, the distance between the left shoulder and the club. The error into which many golfers fall is to allow this arm to collapse at the top of the swing in an attempt to get the clubhead further back. Another way in which golfers feel they are improving the length of their backswing is by releasing control of the club, particularly with the left hand.

We have to reconsider the purpose of the backswing before we can fully appreciate these errors. The ideal backswing sets the club in a position from which it can be swung with as much acceleration as possible on the correct swing path into the back of the ball. In achieving the perfect club position, the body must have coiled sufficiently to build up the power for an accelerating release.

Control and power must work together for the best results and the

optimum position for the club shaft at the top of the backswing is when it is horizontal, paralleling the ground. There are some very supple young players who can move the club back further than this while still maintaining perfect control with the left hand and arm, but they are few and far between and the majority of golfers would do well to be content with a position just short of horizontal.

Each golfer will discover his own position which is the perfect compromise between power and control. That position will be the point beyond which one of the controlling factors, the left heel, the left arm or the left hand will be forced to relinquish that control.

I would far rather see golfers with a shorter than horizontal club position, but a relatively high hand position at the top of the backswing. This will create a long enough clubhead arc to generate the acceleration necessary in the downswing without losing vital control.

AIMING AT THE TOP

A

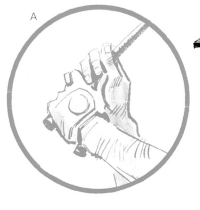

B

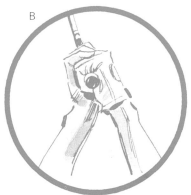

The second vital aspect of the top of the backswing position is the placing of the club in relation to the line of the swing. In discussing the plane of the swing earlier, we saw how the perfect backswing kept the club scraping the under surface of an imaginary sheet of glass resting on the player's shoulders and resting on the ground just beyond the ball at address.

A further look at that position will make it evident that the club which has followed the plane of the swing exactly will be pointing directly at the target at the top of the swing. If the club is laid off, pointing to the left of the target, it means that it has dropped below the plane of the swing. If the club crosses over and points right of the target, it means that the hands have risen above the ideal swing plane. If the club is out of plane at the completion of the backswing, it means that some form of correction is necessary on the way back to the ball or the acceleration of the clubhead will be applied in the wrong direction.

Whenever you are forced into making a mid-swing correction, your chances of making a good shot are drastically reduced. You might do it occasionally, but you certainly will not be able to play consistently in this way. The only way you can check your top of the swing position by yourself is to swing in front of a mirror. This can be misleading because you will almost certainly not swing as freely as you will on a golf course. The best answer is to ask a golfing friend to stand behind you as you hit several shots. He should be able to see clearly whether your club points at the target at the top of the swing. If he spots that you are pointing the club to the left of the target at the top, you will almost certainly have a bowed left wrist position, the hand and club pointing downwards from the end of the left arm. If the club points to the right the bend in the left wrist will almost certainly be the other way, cupping the wrist under the shaft. Obviously both these positions have to be corrected in the downswing before contact is made with the ball. Far better to eliminate them altogether.

club with the last three fingers of the left hand. If these three fingers remain in firm contact with the grip throughout the swing, it is impossible to let the club fall past the horizontal position at the top although an enormously long shoulder turn could just manage it. The reason for trying to aim the club at the target at the top of the backswing is to stay within the basic plane of the swing which we talked about earlier. If the club points right or left of the target line it is outside the plane from the ball through the shoulders and therefore requires a correction at the start of the downswing to approach the ball on the correct swing path.

Mental pictures

What we are trying to achieve here is an overall feeling for the swing. This is extremely important before we move on to discuss your own swing analysis and correction programme in detail. Far too many golfers think only of detailed items within the swing and not at all of an overall swing pattern or thought. It is then that it becomes far too easy to lose sight of the real objectives of the golf swing. That is why I want to take this chance to strengthen your mental picture of the golf swing so that everything we move on to discuss will become corrections within an established overall framework—not just a series of unconnected thoughts leading to ultimate confusion.

It is amazing how much can be achieved in a short time on the practice tee if you set out with a firm plan in mind and work to a logical sequence. Always loosen up the muscles with a few practice swings; always hit a few shots with your feet together to set your rhythm; and always start with the short irons. Only then are you ready to move on to the aspect of the game you are keen to improve. Make a point of getting yourself prepared—if you start cold you will not get far. Have a firm target in mind for every shot on the practice ground—and don't rush.

The grand design

Our understanding of the various factors and forces which operate within the swing must not make us lose sight of the grand design. The golf swing exists to create the simplest way of giving the golf ball a healthy and consistent rap in the back. Whatever we discuss and whatever you experiment with on the golf course, never lose sight in your mind of the wonderfully simple, flowing swing which would achieve all your golfing ambitions. Throughout my golfing life I have carried my father's image of the scythe stroke—a slow placing of the club into position in the backswing and a release of continuous acceleration through the ball. Keep it in mind. You will appreciate the full benefits later.

If you can now accept the proven scientific facts we have discussed about the way the golf ball reacts to the forces which are applied to it, we can combine this absolute knowledge with the way certain parts of the golf swing actually feel. Both are of equal importance. It helps our understanding of the game's technique to know the facts, but it helps us more to put theory into practice by knowing and understanding the feel of the golf club in our hands.

On the practice ground

A swing which is not rhythmical or balanced creates a great feeling of clumsiness. Always remember that comfort will lead to confidence. The first steps in our improvement programme home in on the crucial elements.

Putting theory into practice can be a difficult task for golfers. The key is to establish an understanding of the root causes of the basic swing problems and then to build up a straightforward plan of campaign to overcome these difficulties. But there are no instant cures.

I believe we are now armed with enough information to be able to set out a practice programme based on the analysis we have carried out on your own swing. This is set out in two distinct parts: one for those who hit the ball from left to right in the air, or hit the ball straight left of where they are aiming; and the second for those golfers who hit the ball from right to left in the air or straight to the right of their aiming point.

Anyone who hits the ball to the left and makes it turn even further left, or who hits high, weak shots, should step into line with those who hit it straight left. Any players who start the ball to the right of the target and bend it further right, or who have difficulty in getting the ball into the air, should study section two.

General principles
All the fine details are covered in the illustrations and captions, but here I will outline the general principles of what we are doing. Our starting point, as always, is the head of the club. And as we discovered in chapter one, we can determine the clubface position—open, closed or square—by the way the golf ball moves in the air. Once we know the clubface position, we know the relative position of the hands on the grip of the club. We have also worked out that the positioning of the hands can have an effect on shoulder alignment and therefore on swing line.

We know that the line on which the club is swung sets the initial direction taken by the ball and that the clubface position determines the way it will curve in the air. The first step in our improvement programme is to check your grip. The chances are that it will be wrong if the ball is bending in the air. Adjust the grip until the flight of the ball is straight. Those who bend the ball to the right must move their hands to the right as they grip the club and those who curve the ball from right to left must move their hands to the left. The important thing to remember is that the hands must work as a unit, they must move together. This can be easily checked by releasing the grip on the club and straightening the fingers to see if the palms of the hands are facing each other. Too many things can go wrong in the golf swing without the hands fighting each other all the time.

Balance in the golf swing does not just mean staying on your feet without falling over. It means balance throughout the action—the movement of one leg balancing the other, the backswing balancing the downswing, the position of the hands balancing and complementing each other. Once the ball is flying correctly, then you can begin to incorporate any set-up or posture adjustments you may have found necessary. Once we have the ball moving in a straight line we know from our previous examination that it is moving in the same direction that you are swinging the club. In other words, the flight now matches the swing line. From the direction in which it flies we can determine exactly whether the swing line at impact is from out-to-in or from in-to-out.

Alignment of the body
To a large extent your own natural reactions will take over from this point. If you hit the ball consistently straight left of where you intend it to go you will very soon start to aim more to the right. This, in turn, will automatically start to correct the

alignment of the feet, hips and shoulders and encourage a return to the inside-straight through-inside again swing line.

This is the point, too, where some of the lessons we learned in front of the mirror come into force—ensuring a square set-up and proper posture and checking the relationship between the left arm and the club. A simple way to check alignment on the practice ground is to place a club on the ground pointing at your target. It is then relatively easy to line up squarely to this club.

As soon as you feel you have made the first important step, that you are now hitting the ball straight, we should give some immediate attention to rhythm and balance, for even when the geometry of the swing is correct, the best results can only be achieved with the addition of these two ingredients. Yet they are not easy to define. It is not possible to clarify them as simply and factually as a change in grip position. But they can have just as important an impact. In asking you to analyse your own swing and to understand the various factors which can effect your golf, I have been demanding a great deal of mental effort from you. This has been quite deliberate, because golf is a game which requires a combination of mental and physical factors.

Strength of mind

Moving ball games like tennis also require mental effort in learning various methods and strokes, but once play has started, the speed of the game means that the majority of play is determined by reflex action rather than a careful blend of mental and physical effort. This is where golf is possibly unique—and it is the correct blend, the right mixture, of mind and body which creates success. I strongly believe that rhythm and balance are the twin links between the mental and physical sides of the game and that if these can be achieved they can over-ride anxiety, pressure and frustration to an extent which will allow you to play with some degree of control in even the tightest situations. So how do we set about mastering these elusive elements?

Firstly we must understand that they can be achieved largely through physical effort and that we are not going to be delving into the realms of Buddhism, self-hypnosis, or anything more difficult to understand than the old-fashioned art of concentration. I feel that every golfer, in fact every athlete or sportsman of any kind, should have a set routine which he or she can follow before every shot, every serve at tennis, every race, every throw of the javelin. This routine should put them in the best possible physical position to achieve their aim and should also set their mind in the correct gear. By constant repetition this individual routine will be the means by which the athlete brings his mind and body together at the all-important moment.

I am going to recommend a particular golf routine which I feel you should try. You might eventually decide that it does not quite suit your game or personality and go on to make certain amendments, or perhaps come up with an entirely different routine. But this one is designed to cover all aspects of the physical-mental

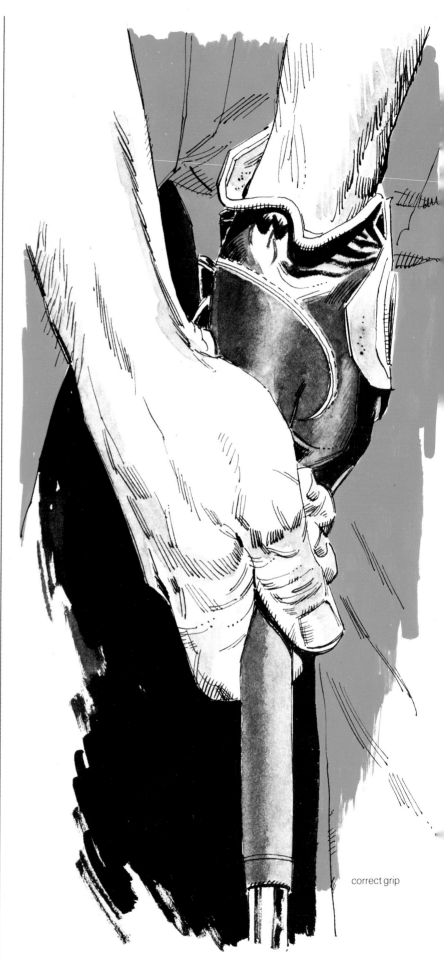

correct grip

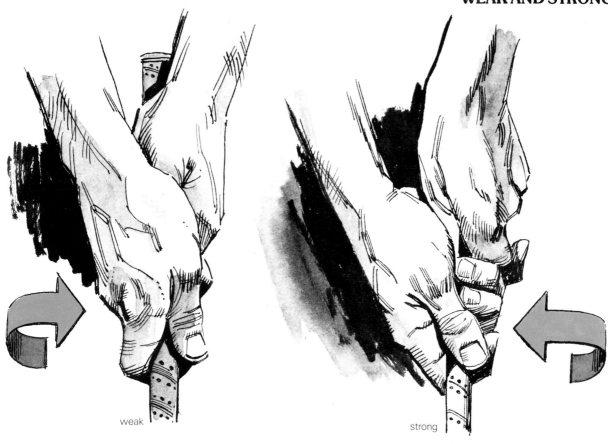

weak

strong

The first objective in our plan to improve your golf is to straighten out the flight of the ball. All the time that your shots bend off to the right of the target your natural instincts will lead you to aim off to the left. This is entirely the wrong thing to do as it increases the basic problem rather than solves it. The same applies to the golfer who hits the ball consistently from right to left. He will quite naturally aim off more to the right, adding to the original fault.

We know that the swing path sets the initial direction of the ball; but it is the clubface position that decides the ultimate flight of the ball. There are two reasons why the clubface may be open or closed at impact rather than square. The grip may be correct, but the hands may be used too little or too much in the swing, leaving the clubface pointing right of the target or turning it over to the left. In the extreme cases it is possible to address the ball with the clubface open and to use the hands to such an extent through the ball that a hook shot results; and to have the clubface closed at address and fail to get the hands into the shot at all, causing a slice. In general terms, however, if the ball bends right or left in the air, the first thing to check is your grip. The chances are very strong that this is where the basic fault will lie.

We show here a good grip, a weak grip and a strong grip as the player will see it, looking down on his hands as he addresses the ball.

Dealing first with our good player whose swing line is on the correct in-to-in path, starting the ball out straight at the target, we will examine his problem when the ball bends consistently off to the right. In checking his grip this player will almost certainly find that his right hand is a little too much on top of the shaft. He should experiment by moving both hands slightly to the right in the grip; hitting a sufficient number of shots on the practice tee to see if the adjustment has been enough to effect a cure.

With shots which start straight and bend to the left the grip adjustment must be in the other direction, moving both hands slightly to the left as he looks down on the grip. No grip change is easy, but for the player swinging the club on the correct line, this adjustment will be the one step necessary to make him a good golfer.

CURING A SLICE

The out-to-in swinger forms the largest category in golf. As we have proved earlier, he can match any one of the three clubface positions – square, open or closed – to produce a pull stright to the left, a slice starting left and bending right or a pull-hook, starting left and going further left.

Very few people will hit the ball consistently to the left of the target in a straight line as they will naturally aim further and further right until they get the ball on target. So the person who combines a square clubface with an out to-in swing will probably straighten himself out fairly quickly. The most common combination is an open clubface with this type of swing and it causes the dreaded, high, weak slice.

Following our correction pattern, we must first make the ball fly straight. Check the grip and almost certainly you will find the hands too far left on the club. Move them to the right until you can regularly hit the ball on a straight line through the air. We know that because you are swinging out-to-in, the ball will now go left of the target and it is here that your natural reactions will help to correct the fault. Automatically, you will aim more to the right and this will bring your foot position back to square and pull round the line of the shoulders to aim just to the left of the target instead of well off to the left. We have also seen how the strengthening of the grip pulls the right shoulder down and back and this will be a corrective factor.

If you start the ball to the

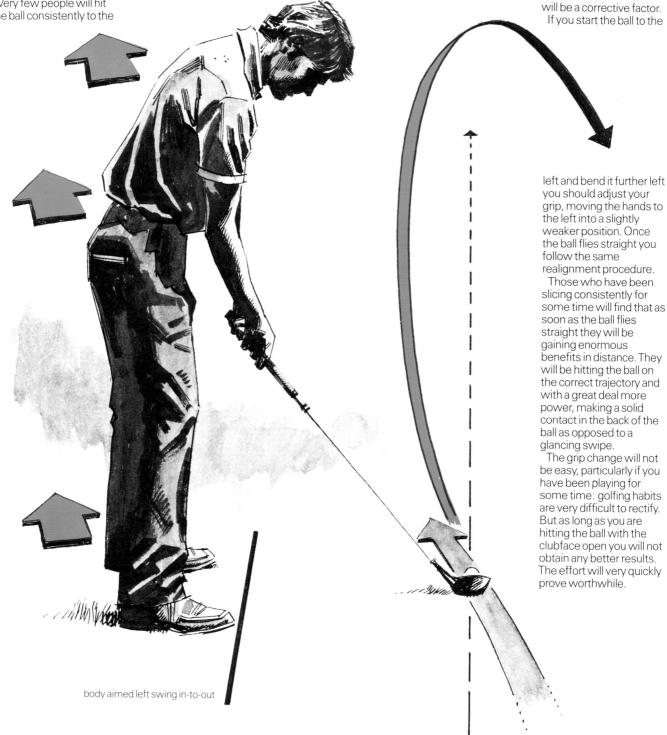

body aimed left swing in-to-out

left and bend it further left you should adjust your grip, moving the hands to the left into a slightly weaker position. Once the ball flies straight you follow the same realignment procedure.

Those who have been slicing consistently for some time will find that as soon as the ball flies straight they will be gaining enormous benefits in distance. They will be hitting the ball on the correct trajectory and with a great deal more power, making a solid contact in the back of the ball as opposed to a glancing swipe.

The grip change will not be easy, particularly if you have been playing for some time: golfing habits are very difficult to rectify. But as long as you are hitting the ball with the clubface open you will not obtain any better results. The effort will very quickly prove worthwhile.

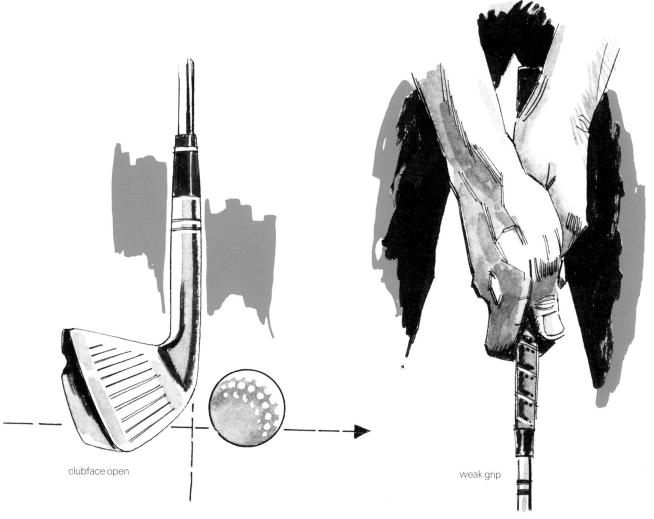

clubface open

weak grip

STRAIGHTENING A HOOK

Those golfers who hit the ball with an in-to-out swing will almost invariably have compensated by aiming off to the right, closing the stance and the shoulder position – and making matters worse.

If this kind of player hits the ball with a square clubface the shots will finish right of the target, but at least will fly straight. The cure is relatively simple and mostly follows your own natural instincts. You must straighten out your alignment, pulling the left foot back into a square position with the right foot and opening up the shoulder line.

The more normal result of an in-to-out swing will be a hook shot, which starts out to the right and bends left of the target. This is because the swing is normally combined with a closed clubface position at impact which imparts hook spin to the ball.

As with all our other swing faults, we must start the road to improvement by making the ball fly straight so that we can clearly see the remainder of the problem. Once again we go straight to the grip as being the most likely culprit. Almost certainly the hands will be too far to the right, the right hand actually creeping under the shaft at times. Remember that the hands must move together when any grip change is taking place, making sure that they are exactly opposite each other and working in unified balance.

Move the hands to the left as you look down at the grip, experimenting on the practice area until you are quite regularly getting the ball moving in a straight line. We have seen already that this grip change will also have the effect of pulling the left shoulder back and down.

This in itself is a step towards correcting the faulty set-up and alignment which you gradually fell into because the ball was constantly bending to the left of where you were aiming. As you now have more control over the flight of the ball, you will be able to aim more directly at the target, getting the feet into a square position and allowing the shoulder line to point just left of the target rather than the right as you have been doing.

If you are unfortunate enough to hit the ball to the right with slice spin taking it further and further away from the green, then your grip adjustment must be to the right, adopting a stronger grip until the ball flies straight. Your realignment procedure will then be the same as for those who hook the ball.

body aimed right

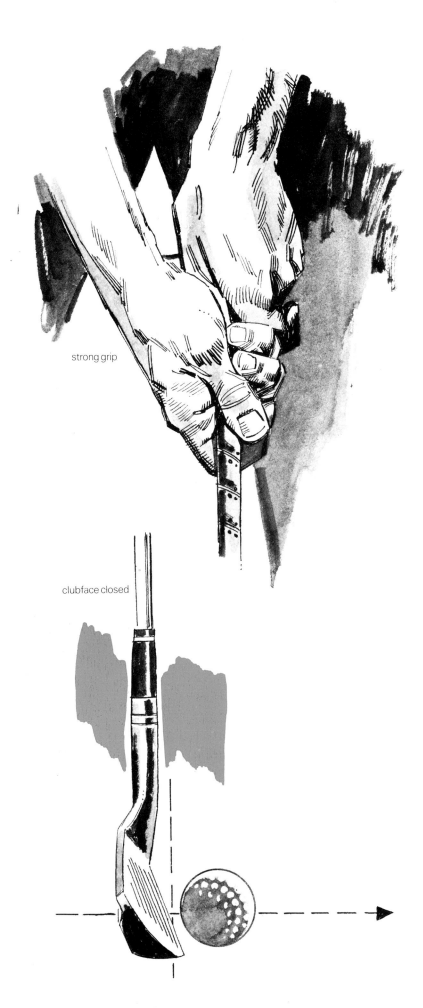

strong grip

clubface closed

combination and the resulting interactions.

First we want to take a critical look at what we expect the shot to achieve. This can best be done by standing behind the ball and looking towards the target—whatever area you have selected for your target. This may be simply the middle of the fairway if you are playing a wedge shot out of deep rough, a section of the fairway short of a bunker to set up a second shot to the green, or you may be aiming straight at the pin if you feel full of confidence or your opponent has laid one really close to the hole. Most of these decisions can be forming in your mind as you approach your ball, weighing up the problems and difficulties you face.

Focus the mind

Once you have made up your mind about the shot and selected the correct club, you should then go into your routine. Stand behind the ball and picture the shot you are about to play. You will find that as you look from the ball to the target and form a mental picture of its flight through the air, you will gradually begin the mental process of closing out the trees, traps or lakes which endanger the shot. Your concentration will focus more and more closely on the ball and the target and it is in this frame of mind that you should place the clubhead behind the ball while gripping the club very lightly. Let the clubhead sit on the ground and only firm up the grip when you have got the whole set up correctly in place. Because you started with a clear mental image of the shot to be played, every small part of this routine will help build your concentration along the right lines. Each step in the routine builds another section of wall between you and the outside world, shutting out all problems and distractions, until, when you are finally ready to start your backswing you are aware only of the ball and the target. Your concentration is being focused down an ever-narrowing cone.

Amateur's shot

The average amateur golfer's approach to each shot is usually the reverse. He has a quick glance towards where he wants the ball to go as he settles into his address position. But this glance will show him more of the problems which surround his target than the target itself. No real concentration is being applied until he looks at the ball at the start of the swing. The step-by-step building of concentration by the use of a simple routine is easy to achieve and can bring amazingly quick results. This brings us neatly back to our twin links between the mental and physical sides of golf—rhythm and balance. It is through the application of these two factors that improved concentration can best be converted to improved golf and a happier day.

We have seen how closely interrelated the physical movements are in golf—how a small change in the grip can alter the clubface position and vary the entire set-up. Just the same applies to rhythm, balance and concentration—a flaw or a change in one can vitally affect the others. So closely linked are rhythm and balance that it is difficult to know exactly where to start. Probably

Now that we have covered the basic technical problems which plague golfers, we can move on to the vital question of rhythm and balance. I feel that these two factors form the link between the mental and physical sides of golf. Balance does not just mean staying on your feet. In the overall context of the golf swing it means the balance of the hands working together, the backswing balancing the downswing – the creation of a well-oiled, fluid swing. Rhythm can be achieved just as well in a fast swing as a slow one. What is important is that the speed of the backswing allows a flow of acceleration from the top of the backswing through impact.

The best practice ground exercise for building rhythm and balance is extremely simple. Stand with the feet virtually together and hit shots with a three-quarter swing. Any attempt to lead the move into the downswing with the shoulders or excessive use of the hands will quickly throw you off balance. From such a narrow stance there is very little margin for error and any swing which is not rhythmical or balanced will create a great feeling of clumsiness.

clubhead off the ground

You will be pleasantly surprised at how far you can hit the ball in this way, without any apparent effort. I recommend that you spend at least ten minutes of every practice session hitting shots in this way and also that you take several practice swings with the feet together before you step on to the first tee at the start of a game. The swing rhythm is also the first thing to desert most golfers at moments of tension and pressure. When you get into a tight situation, therefore take a couple of practice swings with your feet together to re-establish the swing rhythm in your mind.

the most logical approach is to look initially at balance, for it would be almost impossible to achieve balance throughout the swing without having established the correct rhythm on the way.

As I mentioned earlier, balance does not just mean staying on your feet, but there is a wonderful practice ground exercise which will very soon throw you off your feet if you have got things wrong. I would like you to try it as a first step to building rhythm and balance into your game. It not only shows up errors very fast, but is also the best way I know of developing the correct rhythmic balance in golf. I don't know of any other practice exercise which imparts such a positive feeling. All you need do is hit shots from a very narrow stance—so that any false moves, any sense of imbalance in the swing, will be magnified. Place your feet close together and take as full a swing as you can manage—probably a three-quarter backswing will be as far as you will get.

Golfing sins

Any attempt to overpower the swing with the right hand, or to lead the move into the downswing with the shoulders, as so many slicers do in creating their out-to-in swing, will immediately throw you off balance. With such a narrow stance there is almost no margin for error, whereas in a normal swing the wide-spread stance can hide a multitude of sins, although the resulting behaviour of the ball will reveal the mistakes with depressing inevitability.

A swing which is not rhythmical or balanced will create a great feeling of clumsiness in the feet-together exercise. So clearly do you feel the

mistakes in the swing that the body responds very quickly, almost automatically, to self-correct the imbalance. That is why it is such an invaluable exercise.

Tempo and speed

Quite obviously the speed of the swing is a vital part of rhythm and balance. On the professional tour you see as big a variety of swing tempo as you will find anywhere—and there is nothing wrong with that. It would be ridiculous to expect everyone to swing at the same speed. But what might not be obvious at first glance is that the speed of the backswing is a preliminary which counterbalances the throughswing. The two together make a rounded, balanced swing. This is where many club golfers go wrong—the back-swing being so fast that it is not compatible with an accelerating downswing. Put the two together and they are way off balance. In an incorrect swing tempo you will find almost invariably that the fastest part of the action is at the top of the backswing and the start of the downswing. The speed of the hands and the clubhead leaves the rest of the body hopelessly out of position and there is no way that the clubhead can still be accelerating when it hits the ball.

I am not trying to say that there is anything wrong with a fast swing tempo—mine is distinctly on the quick side—but a fast swing must still be a balanced swing. Every one of us has his own natural pace—the way we walk, talk, eat, work. It is a mistake to interfere with this built-in pace-maker. So what we must do is to harness it correctly in relation to our golf. The vital areas of

59

speed control lie in the start of the backswing and the conversion of the backswing into the downswing.

The biggest universal fault is not the overall speed of the swing, but an action away from the ball which is too fast. This is an area which can throw the rest of the swing off balance. I would recommend that you study the action of a pro who moves at approximately the same speed as you do—with luck it will be the same player whose posture we examined in an early part of the book. But if it is a different star who matches your swing tempo it won't make any difference. Watch particularly for the start of the backswing. It may be reasonably fast, but it will always be smooth and it will always allow much greater acceleration from the top of the swing.

Even pace
I mentioned earlier that I felt the club should be placed, not swung, to the top of the backswing, and this is a feeling that will help a lot of golfers with a fast tempo to overcome the quick snatch away from the ball. Jack Nicklaus has one of the most evenly-paced take-away actions in professional golf and it would pay fast and slow swingers alike to watch him. The balance between take-away, backswing and downswing in Jack's relatively slow action is what every golfer should be looking for. This beautiful rhythm is much easier to see in a slow swing, but it doesn't matter how much faster you swing as long as the same balance is there. In fact, Jack has a simple method of ensuring a smooth take-away. He addresses the ball with the clubhead just off the ground. Try it and see how difficult it becomes to snatch the clubhead back from this position. By never allowing the clubhead to touch the ground you get the feeling that the swing has begun even before the clubhead has moved.

Rhythm in the mind
On the practice ground I would suggest that you put this above-ground address position together with your narrow-stance exercise as a double protection against faulty rhythm and balance. Use the feet-together exercise for at least ten minutes during every practice ground session, slowly moving towards a more normal stance as you gain confidence. Whenever you switch to a bigger club, hit the first two or three shots with your feet together to ensure that you start with the correct rhythm. Use it also as a warming-up exercise on the first tee so that you can subconsciously implant a feeling of rhythm in your mind before you attempt your first shot. There is no reason, either, why you should not take a few practice swings with your feet together at regular intervals during the round—even one swing like this before every shot if you feel it is necessary. Anything you can do to achieve rhythm and balance in your golf will pay rich rewards.

Cause and effect
Inevitably in a book of this type we must devote a good deal of time and a certain amount of space to detailed descriptions and analysis of the swing

Another excellent way to establish rhythm in the swing and, in particular, to prevent snatching the clubhead away from the ball, is to copy the example of Jack Nicklaus. He addresses the ball with the clubhead just off the ground, never allowing the club to rest behind the ball. It becomes very difficult to snatch the clubhead away from the ball, as you have the feeling that the swing has begun even before the clubhead has moved. Using this method you are almost forced to take the club

back slowly and evenly from the ball. Even if the overall tempo of your swing is quite fast the first two feet of the backswing must not be rushed.

Once you have had the chance to use your feet-together practice routine a few times and have begun to build up a well-balanced swing, you should try to establish the length and power of

swing which gives you the best results. Warm up thoroughly with ten minutes or so of practice with the feet together. Now take a fairly lofted club in which you have a lot of confidence, perhaps your six, seven or

eight-iron. Hit 20 shots with this club, with your feet together and using no more than a three-quarter swing. Collect the balls and pay particular attention to how closely they are grouped. Leave some sort of marker, a club will do, at the centre of the best group.

With the same club, but using your normal stance and full swing, go through the same routine. Have you gained very much in distance? Are the balls as closely grouped? Try the same thing again, using your normal stance and set-up, but cutting down on the swing slightly, not trying to use full power. Keep experimenting until you have determined what is best for you — whether it means a little extra distance but a loss of accuracy, or whether you prefer to be accurate even if it means giving away a little distance.

Try the same routine with a range of clubs and gradually you will build up a confident swing pattern on which you can depend.

RHYTHM AND BALANCE

and its various component parts. Yet I must emphasise that this is done to increase your understanding of the underlying factors which cause a variety of results. I hope I have explained these factors in such a way that you have a greater and more simple understanding and that I have cleared up many of the seemingly endless complications which can arise in golf. My purpose has been to create a more tangible link between cause and effect in the golf swing so that you will be armed with this knowledge on the course and on the practice ground. This will enable you to analyse and rectify your own problems, not only making you more efficient in terms of technique, but also giving you the confidence to tackle the more difficult shots and making you a stronger all-round competitor. Yet I cannot emphasise too strongly that you should have an overall concept, a mind picture, of the swing. On the golf course you must allow that image and your own natural rhythm to dominate. There is possibly room for one key thought during the swing—no more.

In conclusion

The detailed work has been our preparation for the grand design. That is why the general thoughts and images I have discussed in this chapter are as important as the details which preceeded them—possibly more so. While the learning and understanding can only be achieved through the detailed work, the swing should be viewed as a whole when it comes to putting theory into practice on the golf course.

Closely allied to the twin benefits of rhythm and balance is the art of concentration. I believe this can be encouraged if the golfer goes through a set routine before every shot. As you approach every shot, make a point of studying the problems that lie ahead. As you are walking to your ball on the fairway, you can be studying the trees, traps or lake that will endanger the next shot. By the time you reach the ball, you will have a clear idea in your mind of what you want the shot to do. You should try to develop a clear mental image of the ball in flight, landing on target.

From the time you take

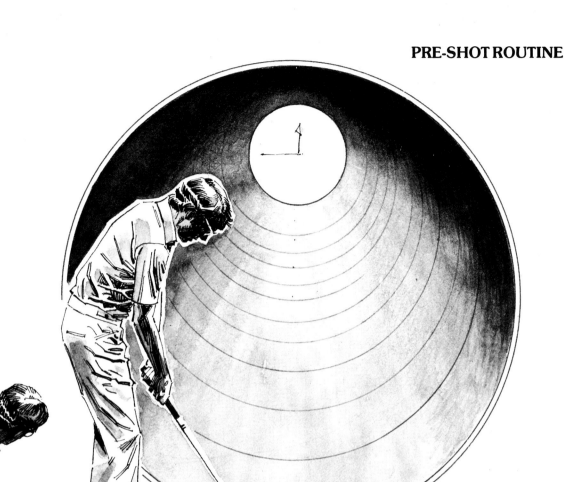

Quantity and quality

There would seem to be a feeling among many players that they can gain some measure of respect from their fellow golfers by hitting the greatest number of practice shots in the shortest time. I must agree that any practice is better than none and that a lot of practice is better than a little – but it must be planned and progressive application, not mindless slogging for the sake of boasting in the club bar. You should always start out with a clear practice plan and preferably start from the beginning with each shot. By this I mean choosing a target, lining up the clubface and taking your proper stance and set-up before hitting the shot. Try not to fall into the habit of standing in one position and pulling the next ball in front of you without going through the set-up routine, for this will become an important part of both the mental and physical preparation for each shot you play.

Care and progress

The next time you head for the practice ground take a good look at the people who have made extra time available to improve their golf. You can almost guarantee that 90 per cent will fire off as many shots in 15–20 minutes as they hit in a normal round of golf. The player who takes care over every shot is almost certainly the man who is making the most progress. He will have improved both his style and his accuracy, as opposed to achieving more length and hitting more golf balls.

the club from the bag you should have considered the problems and decided on your course of action. You should have only positive thought in your mind from this point on. Holding the club lightly in both hands, approach the ball from behind and place the clubhead behind the ball.

Move your feet into a square position and adopt your correct set-up, finally firming up on the grip.

Throughout this time you will be encouraging the mental picture of a successful shot and your attention will be focusing down more and more to the ball and the target. You should be developing a narrowing cone of concentration that will blot out all the dangers which confront the shot, leaving you with a positive mental picture.

The driver and the long game

The aim here is to outline the factors which have a
bearing on hitting the ball a long distance, and to
warn you of the areas where you will possibly lose
accuracy. Remember to build one step at a time on a
solid, proven foundation.

Hitting the ball a long way
is every golfer's ambition.
First we must know what
causes the ball to fly as far
as possible, and then arrive
at a balance between
applying the power and
keeping the ball in play.

Now that we are getting down to specific sections
of the game, we have to take an objective look at
what we are trying to achieve in each department.
Where the long game is concerned there is a
conflict between distance and accuracy. It is
really up to each individual player to decide which
will be most beneficial to him, assuming that he
cannot immediately achieve both. What I aim to
do in this chapter is outline the factors which have
a bearing on hitting the ball a long way and also to
warn you of the areas where you will possibly lose
accuracy.

Our previous studies leave us in no doubt that
the ball flies further and more accurately when
the swing line is directly towards the target at
impact and the clubface is square to the swing
line. Until this state has been achieved there is
absolutely no point in trying for greater distance
because you will be building on a weak base. The
whole thing will crumble around you at the first
moment of crisis, if not before, and your chance of
hitting the ball significantly further or of keeping it
in play will be very slim indeed. You can't take
short cuts in this game. You can only build, one
step at a time, on a solid foundation of proven
fundamentals.

Applying power
The next thing to understand is exactly what
causes the ball to fly a long way. Going back once
again to the simplest possible terms, it can only be
the impact between club and ball which can make
one shot fly further than another. We have
proved that swing line, clubface alignment and
the angle at which the club attacks the ball are
vital. It doesn't take a mental giant to see that the

only other factor which can affect the clubhead
impact on the ball is the amount of power being
applied. And here lies an inherent problem, for
large numbers of golfers cannot appreciate that
the only way to impart more power to the golf ball
is to move the clubhead faster.

Can you imagine a 100-ton locomotive travelling at a steady 20mph being in collision with a
golf ball. You know instinctively that the ball
would not travel very far. Yet if that same golf ball
is in collision with a 13-ounce driver being swung
at 120mph by Tom Weiskopf we know very well it
will not come back to earth until it has covered
more than 260 yards. There is no way that even
Tom can wield the same power as a train, but he
can certainly make a golf ball fly—because of the
speed he generates in the head of the club.

Clubhead speed
Some golfers are better equipped to generate
clubhead speed than others, but it is not an
essential requirement to be built like a
heavyweight champion. Many smaller players hit
the ball extremely long distances. Look at Chi Chi
Rodriguez from Puerto Rico. He is very small and
light, yet has been known to hit the ball past all of
the recognised big hitters. His great asset is his
ability to move the clubhead fast at the right
moment—and that means building up the speed
in continuous acceleration from the top of the
backswing. There is no way that a fast backswing
can produce greater clubhead speed at impact, as
we have proved in our rhythm tests.

Now we are narrowing the problem down even
more. Clubhead speed created between the top
of the backswing and impact—nowhere else. It

comes about as a result of latent power built up in the backswing and that power creates momentum to convert the backswing into the downswing. Why is it that some people can increase their clubhead speed more than others in this part of the swing? It depends a great deal on the correct positioning of the body from address. For instance, the golfer who adopts a very closed stance, aiming to the right of his target, will not be able to swing the clubhead through the impact area towards the green because the left side of his body will be in his way. You must be in a position to allow the club to swing freely past the body in order to obtain clubhead speed. On the other hand, a very open stance can often lead to an out-to-in swing and we have seen this hits the ball with a glancing blow and is no way to achieve longer, more powerful shots.

You can see now why I stressed certain fundamentals in the golf swing which cannot be varied if you intend to play good golf. Time and time again we come across situations in the game of golf where we realise that good results can only be achieved if our efforts are correctly allied to the key basics. Assuming that our stance and set-up allows us to move the clubhead fast in the right direction, what else can we do to boost clubhead speed? There is only one factor left which we have not covered—the length of the swing arc from the top of the backswing to the ball. If the effective acceleration of the clubhead takes place between these two points it follows that the greater the distance between these points, the greater the exploitable area for increasing acceleration.

Extending the arc

We have seen how shorter golfers automatically stand further away from the ball and therefore swing on a flatter plane than the taller player. This effectively gives them the longest swing arc of which they are capable, although it can't create as big an arc as the bigger player has at his disposal. But both short and tall golfers have the opportunity to increase their swing arc by getting their hands into the highest possible position at the top of the backswing. Any extension of the swing must be tackled sensibly and in a logical fashion. Let me prove the point with a few practice swings which will demonstrate the ways in which some people set about hitting the ball further. You don't need a ball for this and you can do it in your own back garden, maybe even in the house.

Swing the club back until your hands have reached shoulder height only. Now relax your grip on the club until the clubhead falls down around your left shoulder. This is the idea some people have for a big swing and, hopefully, a big hit. Certainly the clubhead has a long arc of travel from behind the left shoulder to the ball, but the lack of control in the grip will not allow proper acceleration and it will also lead to lack of consistency at impact and loss of accuracy.

Let's start again and take the hands back to shoulder height in the backswing. Keeping more control over the grip, push your hands up as far as your hip and body turn will allow, while keeping the right elbow relatively close to the body and

FIRM LEFT SIDE

A key factor in the long game is the dominance of the left side. In the swing sequence on these and the next two pages the firm control of the left side can be clearly seen from address to the top of the backswing and half way into the downswing before the power of the right side becomes apparant.

I always have the feeling that the guiding left side is balancing the power of the right and personally I give no thought to the right side at all for it is strong enough to play its natural part. What is important is that emphasis is given to the left side so that it is not overpowered by the right.

Balance in the golf swing is more than just a question of remaining nicely poised on your feet. There are balancing factors throughout the swing and the most important in the long game is this balance

between the guiding left side and the powerful right. Any naturally left-handed person who plays golf right-handed has a distinct advantage.

Notice the firm relationship between the left arm and shoulder and the club at take-away, halfway back and at the top of the swing. This relationship is maintained as the backswing converts to the acceleration of the downswing and then you can see the power of the right hand and side really working into the shot. Even at impact the left arm is exerting its guiding influence as the clubhead sweeps through on a shallow arc into a full finish.

RELEASING THE POWER

Also clearly shown is the weight transference at the start of the downswing from the inside of the right foot to the outside of the left. It is often useful to repeat a short phrase to yourself during shots like these in order to establish the rhythm and timing without which the shots would not work. If you are concentrating on the weight shift into the downswing you could repeat 'inside right . . . outside left' to yourself as you move into the backswing and then accelerate back to the ball.

It is vital to get the rhythm and the balance of the swing working in unison to get the best results from the long game. Don't be tempted to rush at the shot because you have a long club in your hands. Complete the backswing and hit the ball at your normal pace. The length of the shaft and the loft of the clubface will do the rest.

ensuring that it points down towards the ground. This 'stretch' position at the top of the backswing is a key factor for all big hitters. It increases the swing arc considerably without surrendering control over the club. There is, however, an error which can wipe out all the advantage you might gain from this position. In stretching for a big turn some golfers will allow the left heel to lose all effective contact with the ground, destroying the power build-up as we have seen. In this respect I personally allow my left heel to raise an inch or two off the ground in order to achieve a slightly bigger turn for full shots from the driver to the five-iron. But this in no way lessens my firm contact with the ground or throws away the control which is essential in the big shots.

This is where we come back to the evergreen question—distance or accuracy? I would have to say that each golfer must make up his own mind because factors beyond the length of his tee shot are involved. For instance, a booming drive at a par-four hole will leave you with only an eight-iron to the green, whereas your normal drive means a five or six-iron second shot. But the key question is whether you can hit the green with an eight-iron out of the rough if you miss the fairway with the bigger hit. Are you a strong enough short game player out of the rough to take advantage of hitting the ball 20 or 30 yards further? If not then you are much better to stick to hitting the fairway.

Arnold Palmer has always played the game with flamboyant disregard for danger—possibly because he is uniquely equipped to cope with any situation, many of them seemingly impossible. Young Spaniard Severiano Ballesteros has been made in the same mould. Palmer always advocated hitting the ball hard and then learning to control it. Other eminent players recommend control first and an increase in power as confidence is built up. Arnold's theory is obviously conditioned by his own confidence. 'If I can see it I can hit it. And if I can hit it I can hole it,' he once said about shots out of the most diabolical positions.

Developing confidence

The point I am making is that for Arnold Palmer and most of the powerful tournament professionals it is no real problem to make recovery shots out of the rough. Therefore they have more confidence in making powerful tee shots and consequently they hit the fairway more often. But if a visit to the rough is disastrous for you, then you are obviously much better off keeping the ball in play and forsaking a little distance. There are clearly holes on your course where you would not take chances off the tee and others where it can make sense to try for a longer drive. Yet I don't believe the course is any place to experiment, trying to hit one or two shots outside your normal powers in the course of a round. Develop your ability and your confidence on the practice ground.

Golf is a compromise between hitting fine shots and making as few errors as possible. It is not a game where you need maximum power all the time and, in fact, many professionals will not hit more than half-a-dozen full power shots in a

CONTROL POINTS

The conflict between distance and accuracy in the long game can cause problems for those who have not yet mastered both. There are certain limits within which you can work to get the maximum power without spraying balls all over the golf course.

We have already discussed the length of the backswing and the important part played by the feet in anchoring the swing. There are two or three further detailed points to be considered in specific relationship to the long game. When reaching for a high hand position at the top of the swing – while ensuring that the left arm remains relatively straight and that the left hand retains its grip on the club – it is vital to ensure that the right elbow stays as close to the side of the body as possible and that it points down towards the ground. There can sometimes be a tendency to allow the elbow to fly away from the side of the body and this destroys the relationship between the arms and the body. It means that a compensatory move of the right elbow back towards the body must be made at the start of the downswing and any extra move is an extra chance to make a mistake.

Another important checkpoint at the top of the swing is the position of the left wrist in relation to the arm and the club shaft. Ideally the left wrist and arm should form a straight line. It should not be cupped under the shaft of the club or bowed the other way. The straight wrist maintains the relationship between the left side and the club that was set up at the address. Take up your normal address position with the left hand, wrist and club forming virtually a straight line. Now bend the left wrist back and then bow it the other way and see what a drastic effect it has on your set-up. This is another built-in error we want to keep out of the swing for we have already seen that it leads to the ciubshaft being aimed off right or left of the target at the top of the backswing.

While stressing the importance of the feet maintaining their firm relationship with the ground during the backswing, I personally allow the left heel to raise between one and two inches to allow a slightly bigger turn for full shots from the driver to the five-iron. With the shorter clubs I keep the heel firmly on the ground.

round. It is a game for thought and planning. Use every element of your ability to achieve the best results and improve that ability by understanding more about the technique of the swing and practising it properly.

Swing technique for the long shots is basically that which applies to the whole game and we have already looked at my overall thoughts in an earlier chapter. Specifically the long shots must be hit with power and control and focussing attention on the left side can go a long way to achieving this ideal. The generally weaker left side of a right-handed person sets the path and the arc of the swing and should prevent the stronger right side from overpowering the swing at impact. We are back to the question of balance—the guiding left side balancing the power of the right. Those who are naturally left-handed and play golf right-handed have a distinct advantage. With a square address position and the weight evenly balanced between the insides of the feet, the left-hand grip should be reasonably firm, particularly in the back of the hand, retaining a controlling grip on the club with the last three fingers. The left arm, hand and club should form virtually a straight line to the ball and this left side relationship should be retained throughout the first 12-18 inches of the take-away, which should be low and almost straight back from the ball. The left arm remains at full stretch in the backswing, and as the hips and body turn to the right the major part of the weight moves to the inside of the right foot, forming a solid base around which the body turns. Ideally the club should point at the target at the top of the backswing and should not fall below a horizontal position.

There are two check points at the top of the swing that you can look out for in practice. The left wrist should form a straight line with the left forearm, not cupped under the shaft or bowed the other way, and the right elbow should be pointing down.

Placing the clubhead
The downswing starts with a movement of weight from the inside of the right foot to the outside of the left. With the knees comfortably flexed at address and through the backswing they will follow the lead given by the feet. The feeling should be that the left side is leading and guiding the swing. No thought need be given to the right side as it is strong enough to play its natural part as long as it is given a firm lead by the left. Failure to concentrate on the left side will almost certainly allow the right to come too much into play, overpowering the swing.

The other key thought to have in your mind while practising these shots is that the hands and the feet should also be balanced—that the weight shift in the feet leads the hands into impact. Above all, these long shots should not be rushed. Remember that the club is placed in position at the top of the backswing and that acceleration starts from there. It is the tendency to rush into long shots which causes many

Five pairs of eyes are following the flight of Hale's shot, as the ball flies into the green.

WOODS, IRONS AND CLUB WORK

Given the choice of hitting a long shot to the green with a five-wood or a two-iron, the vast majority of club golfers would unhesitatingly reach for the wood. The reason is not hard to determine. The thin, long blade of the two-iron does not appear to have sufficient weight and mass to hit the ball very far unless it is hit very hard. Yet the five-wood has a nicely contoured shape and size which creates a feeling of confidence. You might be interested to know that the loft of the five-wood and the two-iron are virtually identical in most sets of clubs. There is very little difference in the weight either; the two-iron is slightly heavier.

This proves quite conclusively that the mental approach to golf is just as important as the scientific. There is no factual reason why the wood is easier to use than the long iron. It is important to remember in every aspect of the game that golf is a blend of fact and feel and there can be no substitute for a club which looks and feels correct to the individual golfer.

If you feel confident of your ability to hit the ball reasonably well with a fairway wood, but far less able to guarantee results with the long irons, then it makes sense to use the woods. But this should not stop you trying to improve your long iron play on the practice ground for it is a skill which will bring its own reward.

Perhaps part of the reason for such a great deal of poor long iron play is that players only pull these clubs from the bag when the majority of the factors which govern each shot are aginst them. If you seldom hit a two or three-iron shot, do not try to dig a half-buried ball out of semi-rough when faced with a 180-yard carry to the green. In addition to the mental pressures which you will face with this club you have loaded the practical and physical dice against yourself before you start.

Try to be sensible about the way in which you select the long clubs for the shot you face. A club like the five-wood will give excellent results from semi-rough, but don't expect it or the long-irons to work miracles from heavier rough. If the ball is sitting well down you must know when to play for safety with a shorter iron. This may well depend on the type of match you are playing. In match play, with your opponent in a commanding position, you may be tempted to try a long-iron shot from a tough position. But if you are trying to protect a medal score or your opponent is also in trouble, then you must use sound judgement and get the ball back into the fairway in order to give yourself a clear shot to the green.

The fairway woods and long irons will give excellent results if played with rhythm and correct technique, but clear thinking and good judgement are also necessary if you are to get the greatest benefit from these clubs.

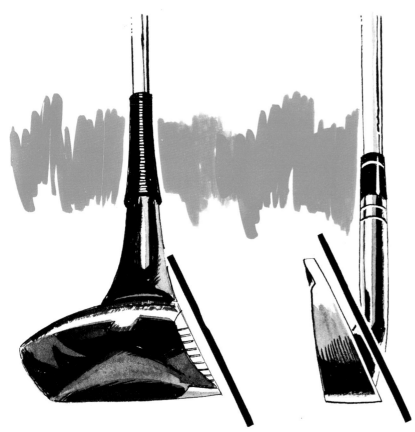

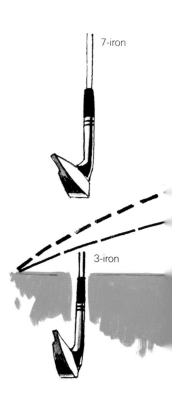

7-iron

3-iron

of the problems for club golfers, particularly with the long irons. I would like you to try a practice ground exercise to prove to yourselves that an even swing tempo is all that is required to hit the ball reasonable distances with these clubs.

Reverting back to our feet-together stance, hit a few relaxed six-iron and seven-iron shots. Using the same swing rhythm hit shots with the three-iron, without trying to hit the ball any further than with the shorter clubs. With the same amount of effort and the same rhythm you will find the ball flying, quite naturally, on a lower trajectory and a little further. It does not take many shots like this to convince you that the long irons will do the job for which they are designed if you will just be content with swinging them in the same way you would a seven-iron. Once you can overcome this mental fear of the long-irons and realise the benefits of swinging them evenly and rhythmically you will be well on the way to adding a new weapon to your golfing armoury. However, there is an alternative. Many golfers prefer to use four and five-woods which have much the same loft as the long irons, but generate more confidence with their more generous clubhead proportions. Whichever clubs you use, the key to the long shots is even-paced rhythm.

There have been many occasions when championships have been won on tight or fast-running courses by players who have had the strength of mind to plan their strategy. If the game was based purely on power the biggest hitters would win every tournament. They don't. So use your long-game skills wisely.

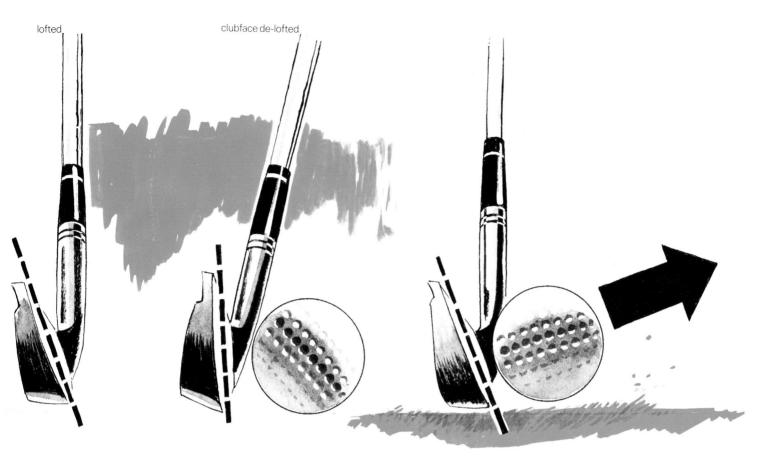

lofted

clubface de-lofted

The angle at which the club approaches the ball — the angle of attack — is nowhere more vital than with the long irons. If your angle of attack is a little too steep with an eight-iron, you will probably hit the shot with the effective loft of a six-iron. Deloft a three-iron to the same extent and you will have trouble getting the ball off the ground at all.

Long irons must be swept into the ball on a shallow angle of attack. Unfortunately many golfers, in their anxiety

and deliver a steep, downward blow. The resultant lack of clubface loft explains their poor result.

Perhaps the best way to prove to yourself that the loft of a three-iron is quite sufficient to get the ball into the air if struck properly, is to play a few lengthy chip shots with this club. Sit the ball on some lush grass, so that you can make good, clean

contact, and try a few crisp chip shots. In this way you should quickly prove to yourself that the club does not need any extra help in getting the ball into the air. The loft on the face is quite enough.

Perhaps one of the easiest methods of developing a feel for long iron shots is to hit them in exactly the same way as you would a seven-iron. Go through your practice tee routine of hitting short iron shots with your feet close together. Get yourself to the point where you are hitting the ball easily and rhythmically. Now switch to a three-

iron and try to hit a few shots with the same feeling as with the seven-iron. Make no attempt to hit long shots or to thrash at the ball. Merely try to hit the ball the same distance as with the shorter iron and with the same easy pace. You will find that the ball does, in fact, travel further and on a lower trajectory.

Handling the long irons in this way, getting the feel of the clubs, learning not to rush into the ball, will slowly build your confidence in their use. Gradually you can take a slightly longer backswing and move the feet further

apart. As soon as you feel you are out of rhythm and are hitting the ball badly, go back immediately to the seven-iron and start again to build up your tempo and your confidence.

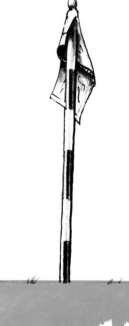

The medium and short game

Accuracy is the name of the game, power does not have a role to play. There is no pride to be gained in hitting the green with as little club as possible. Keep a check on your timing by developing a mental metronome.

Once you move into this area of golf there is no possible confusion about the overriding aim. Accuracy is the name of the game—and it makes no difference whether you achieve that accuracy with a six or an eight-iron. Power plays no part. I always feel that from the five-iron down the amateur player has every chance to make his biggest impression in golf. Yet, surprisingly, you will see amateurs hammering away with the driver on the practice ground when a little work with the medium and short irons would almost certainly pay bigger dividends. There is also the unfortunate tendency for some players to power the ball with the shorter clubs, thereby often destroying the purpose of this part of the game. I feel a lot of amateurs would be amazed at the clubs many big-hitting professionals use for the shorter shots.

Pick the right club

I know you see on television and read in the newspapers how so-and-so touring professional knocked it on to the green at a 170-yard par-three with a seven-iron. For a start there will certainly have been a strong following wind—and why do you suppose the shot attracts so much attention? That's right—because it is very unusual, not the normal run of things on tour. So why try to swing yourself out of your shoes every Saturday to copy a big-hitting pro who got lucky with half a gale in his favour? What you didn't see was that four holes later, across the wind he took that same seven-iron for a 130-yard shot in order to finesse the ball close to the hole. No pro takes pride in reaching the green with as little club as possible. We are all pleased to get the ball close to the pin with whatever club we have decided to use for the job. How do we set about it?

In our general swing routine and our discussions on the long game we have already covered half of the problem—hitting the ball in the right direction. The other half is hitting it the right distance. Have you noticed how accurate you have become on the practice ground while hitting shots with your feet together. This is because your rhythm and balance are right and there is no pressure on you to hit the ball a long way, because you don't expect the ball to go far from this stance. But just think back to your last round of golf and make a mental note of how many short or medium iron shots you left wide or short of the green. If you had stood with your feet together and made sure you had enough club in your hands, would you have done better? Quite possibly you would. This is a clear indication that you don't need power for this aspect of the game and that it is not really essential to turn into a full backswing position. A three-quarter controlled swing will almost certainly give you more consistent results. Yet you must avoid the trap of shortening your rhythm when you shorten the swing. Whatever the length of the shot you are playing and whatever corresponding length of backswing you employ, you must always retain the rhythm you have established. What you really need is your own mental metronome to keep a constant check on your timing.

Subconscious timing

One way to help achieve this is to repeat a couple of key words to yourself as you swing. These should be linked to a positive swing thought and repeated on the practice ground

Once you get into the range of the medium and short irons there is only one clear objective in view— getting the ball as close as possible to your target. Whatever club achieves that aim is the right one for you.

and during play until you have a subconscious timing device. If, for instance, you have been concentrating on my belief that the downswing starts with a shift of weight from the inside of the right foot to the outside of the left, then your mental trigger might be 'inside right . . . outside left', saying the first part as you wind up in the backswing and the second part at the moment you start back down to the ball. Ideally the first part should have a fairly lazy sound and the second part much more crispness. Should you be concentrating on placing the clubhead at the top of the backswing before accelerating to impact the right key words would probably be 'place and . . . hit'. You can, of course, use any phrase which suits you, adjusting its length and rhythm until you have it absolutely right. The problem with a shorter swing is that it can so easily become a decelerating swing. Even though you are not looking for power, the contact between club and ball must be crisp and firm.

As I have said before, every golf shot must be hit with an accelerating swing. If you are to get the ball to fly correctly, with the proper amount of backspin and control, there must be a firm, decisive impact. Only by this means will you achieve consistent results. A decelerating swing will not allow you to hit the ball the same way every time and will not produce repetitive shots.

Staying cool

The other great pitfall which catches many professionals as well as amateurs, especially under pressure, is an attempt to guide the ball—almost a feeling of trying to place the ball on the green with the hands. Almost inevitably this leads to blocking or pushing the ball out to the right because the hands have tried to hold the clubface on line towards the target instead of releasing to move the clubface fast into the ball. You must be confident that your set-up and alignment are such that the ball will finish on target without the need to guide or push the shot into position. Any doubts or worries and the hands will tighten, causing a weak push shot right and short.

This essential confidence can only be built up with practice and play. It can be a vicious circle—the more greens you miss, the less confidence you have and the tighter you become. You will not be able to release the clubhead freely into the ball and you will miss more greens . . . and lose more confidence . . . but it can work the other way. Every shot you hit on target will boost your confidence a little. The more confident you become in your ability to hit the green, the more you will aim and release the clubhead towards the target. The more you are able to aim and release, the more greens you will hit and the more confidence you will have.

Start on the practice ground with your feet together and really get the feel of the six, seven, eight and nine-irons. Once you are thoroughly relaxed and making good contact, hit a dozen or so shots with the nine-iron using your correct stance. Unless you have made far more progress than I imagined, some of these shots will not be as good as you would wish, others will be average and perhaps one or two almost perfect. Pace off

One of the biggest frustrations in golf is to watch a perfectly hit shot to the green cover the flag all the way and pitch 20 yards short. Knowing how far you hit the ball with the scoring clubs and being able to judge the distance between you and the green are two fundamental factors in good golf.

It is a constant surprise that even people who have been playing golf for many years have no clear idea of the distance they hit the ball with the medium and short irons, or any real conception of the difference between one club and the next. No wonder so many people hit their best shots short of the green. It is up to each individual golfer to establish the distance he can comfortably hit the ball with the scoring clubs. Half an hour on the practice ground is all that is required.

Go through your normal warm-up routine of hitting balls with the feet together until you have firmly established your rhythm. After ten minutes or so you should be relaxed and hitting the ball with a nice, easy action, not trying to force extra distance. Starting with the wedge, hit a dozen shots towards a definite target. Concentrate on accuracy rather than distance. Walk forward and examine your grouping. Discount the

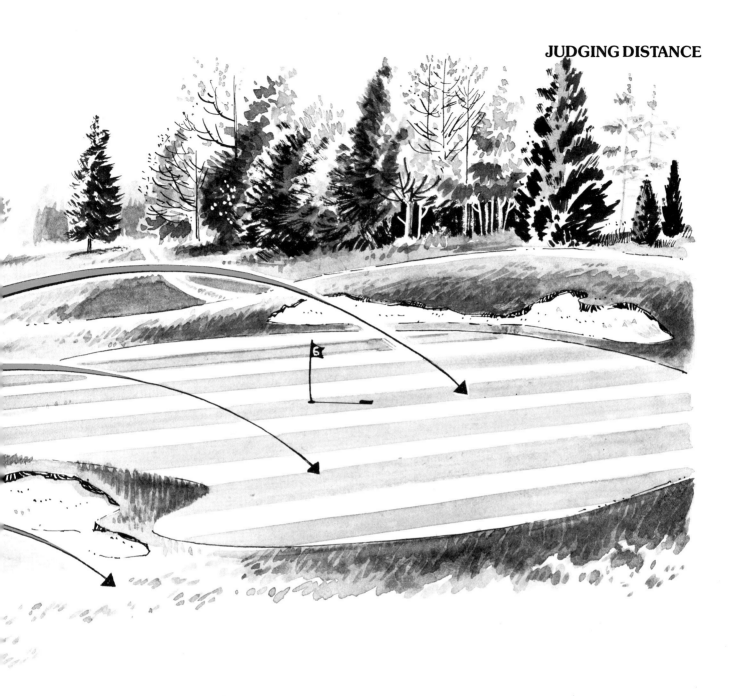

really good and the really poor shots and put your club down in the middle of the area covered by your shots. Go back to the same starting point and go through an identical routine with the nine, eight and seven-irons. Remember that accuracy is the aim of the exercise and any time that you feel you are losing your essential rhythm you should take a few swings with your feet together until you are back in the groove.

When you have completed your shots with each of the four clubs you should pace off the distance that you hit the wedge and then measure the differences between one club and the next. Usually this will be a fairly constant step up, but it doesn't matter what the gap is as long as you know it and it repeats regularly. My club differential is a constant ten yards, until I get to the six, seven and eight irons when the gap becomes 15 yards. The important thing is to know your own capabilities.

You must also be careful to avoid thinking that each of your paces equals one yard. Take the trouble to measure out five of your paces across the carpet at home (they will probably add up to four yards) so that you have an accurate conversion of your capabilities.

It is worth going through this routine at regular intervals, especially if you are working hard to improve your game. As the quality of your striking improves you will tend to hit the ball further.

Having worked out your own personal distance guide you are now in a position to hit the shots which you need to reach the target, ignoring your partners and opponents. If you can hit the ball close to the pin with a six-iron it doesn't matter if the other members of your fourball are hitting nine-irons. Let them worry about their own games, you are beginning to make yours work to its best advantage.

A great temptation for many players is an effort to scoop the ball into the air with the shorter irons. They have the impression that to get the ball high they must somehow get the clubface under the ball and help lift it into the air. Nothing could be further from the truth. Scooping will lead to hitting turf behind the ball or to making contact with the top half of the ball only.

The manufacturers of golf clubs spend vast amounts of money and time on research in an effort to perfect their equipment. There is no reason why they would produce short irons which required the golfer to change his whole concept of the game to hit the ball with an upswing as opposed to a downswing. The reason why top professionals get such a degree of control over the short shots, spinning the ball back once it has pitched on the green, is because they make contact with a still descending clubface, clipping a divot out of the turf once the ball is on its way. This very crisp downward contact imparts maximum backspin to the ball.

If you watch the pros on the practice tee at a tournament, you will notice that they place each ball immediately behind the divots they have taken out with their previous shots. In this way they progress steadily backwards, clipping a neat shape out of the turf. A club golfer with a poor short game would not be able to match this neat symmetry because he would not be consistently taking turf from just under the ball with a downward blow.

the distance to the middle of the group of balls and leave a club on the ground at this point. Now hit another batch of balls with the eight-iron and go through the same procedure. Then do the same with the seven and six-irons.

The information you have now gathered is your own personal guide to more accurate golf. You know how far you hit four of the scoring clubs and, equally important, you know the difference in distance between one club and the next. With most golfers the difference between clubs will be fairly constant. It can be as little as six or seven yards with some players or as much as 15 yards with others. The average will be somewhere about 10 or 12 yards.

Trial and error

The next problem is how to put this knowledge to best use on the golf course. Just how do you learn to judge distance without holding up everyone's game by pacing from ball to green? In a way the average club golfer is lucky in this respect as he plays the majority of his golf on his home course and therefore has an excellent opportunity to see the effect of various shots over the same ground. From the same spot last Sunday you were short with an eight-iron, so this week you give it a try with the seven. This trial and error method will gradually, if you apply yourself to the subject, give you a feeling for distance. You will be able to say with some certainty that you have the right club in your hand for the shot you are about to play—and this is another factor in confidence building. You have all seen players, unsure if they have enough or too much club,

failing to make solid contact because the doubt in their minds would not allow them to release the clubhead through the ball.

There are certain simple guidelines which will help you judge distance more accurately and hopefully get you away from the type of situation I see so often in pro-am events—the player who steps onto the tee at a par-three hole and declares loudly: 'I always hit a seven here.' If golf was really that simple I would be a multimillionaire and you wouldn't be reading this book. Unfortunately there are many factors involved in club selection other than your own particular swing—principally the weather. On exposed courses like those in Britain for the Open Championship you can hit a three-iron one day into the teeth of the wind and the next day the same hole plays downwind with a comfortable eight-iron. This quite emphatically makes the point I am trying to put across. Never prejudge a golf shot. Only when you are standing by the ball can you possibly select the right club for the shot.

How much allowance should you make for the wind? As a general rule a fresh head wind will add one club to the shot and a fairly strong wind might add two clubs. If it blows harder than this you should be considering different types of shot, which we will cover later in the section on trouble. However, it is very difficult to impose hard and fast rules because the effect of wind is different in some parts of the world. In the southern states of America I would say that the wind probably has only half the effect on the ball as the same strength of wind in Britain. This can be caused by the amount of moisture in the air and I know

Any golfer who tries to scoop the ball into the air will take no divots at all. On the practice ground scrape a line on the turf and place the ball exactly on the line. When hitting shots with the medium and short irons any divot which starts before this line is losing you a certain amount of impact control. The clubface must make contact with the ball before it clips the turf. This is the main reason why a short-iron shot hit by a professional will stop very quickly on the green, whereas one hit by a handicap golfer will run on a long way after it pitches.

In order to create the right contact between club and ball it can be helpful to think of accelerating the clubhead to a point six inches past the ball. This helps to keep the club moving right through the ball and is particularly useful on those shots which do not require a full swing.

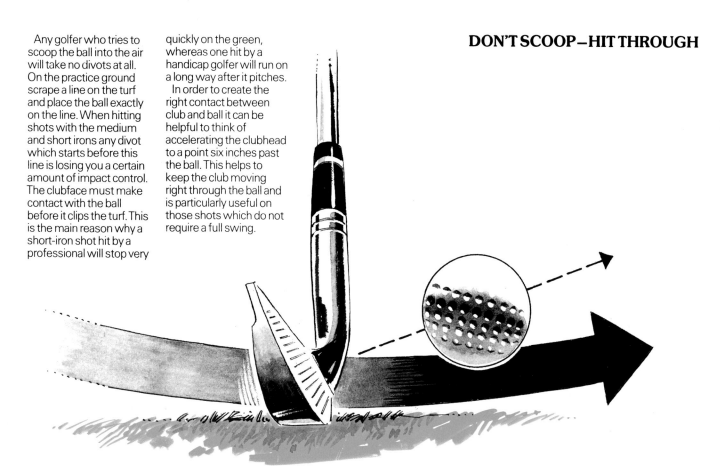

Positioning the ball correctly for a range of shots from the driver down to the wedge causes problems for many golfers. Most of the confusion arises because the stance itself changes from shot to shot and it is difficult for golfers to find a stable point around which to base the ball position.

There are some schools of thought which believe that the ball should be played opposite the left heel for every shot. Personally, I feel that it must move back slightly for the shorter shots because you are hitting a more downward blow than with the driver which is sweeping the ball forward. However, this does not mean that we should ignore the left heel, for it is the one constant factor in the stance.

As the clubs get shorter so the ball, quite naturally, moves closer to the feet and so the right foot moves closer to the left, narrowing the stance. It also moves slightly forward, opening the stance for the short shots. As you look down from your set-up position these three changes give the impression that the ball is now being played from quite well back in the stance, fairly close to the right foot. Yet in reality it is still only just inside the left heel.

On the basis that the left heel retains its position for all shots and that the right moves to the left and forwards, it makes absolute sense to judge all ball placements in relation to the left heel.

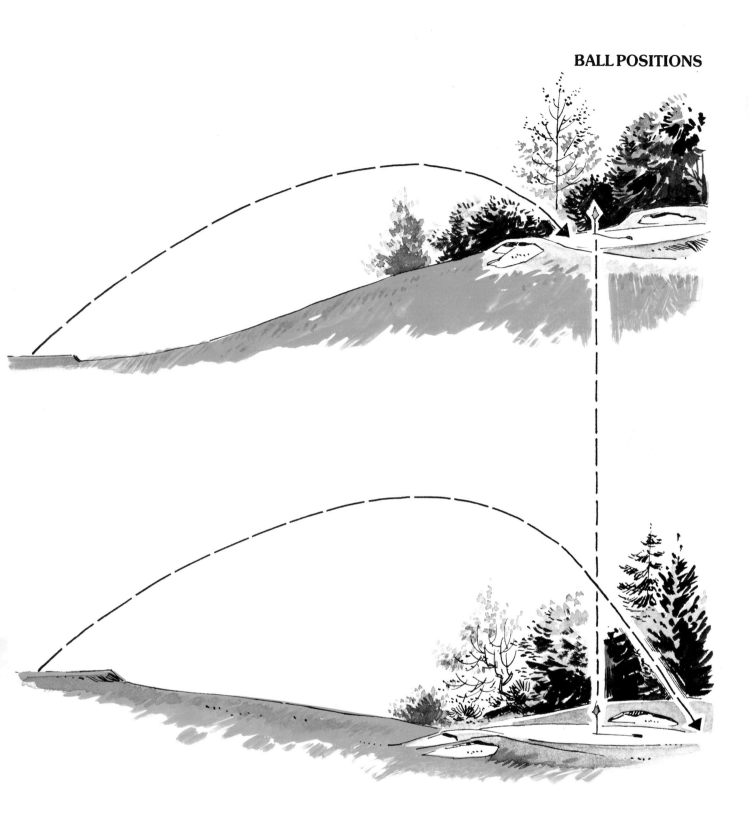

Playing up to a raised green or firing downhill to a target well below you makes the judgement of distance very difficult. In playing to an uphill target, the trajectory of the shot is effectively cut short by the rising ground. Yet when playing downhill, the ball will be in the air longer and therefore the same trajectory will carry it further.

As a general rule, uphill shots will require one club more than for the same distance where ball and target are on the same level. When playing downhill, one club less than normal is a good guide. Uphill shots often tempt a golfer into trying to help the ball to reach the necessary height – the scoop shot with which we have already dealt. Resist this temptation, we have already proved that the loft of the club is all that is required, just so long as it is combined with a crisp, rhythmical downward blow.

many Britsh golfers, used to their own natural conditions, who cannot believe how far the ball will fly against the wind in warmer climates. Another factor which has a big effect on club selection is playing to a green higher or lower than your position in the fairway. You can usually count on needing one more club when playing uphill and one less when playing down.

You quite often find holes where the green is raised and as you line up the shot there is no background behind the putting surface to give you any guide to distance. This can be extremely deceptive and will give the impression of the green being further away than it is in reality. In this situation try to get a clear image of the size of the pin and imagine a person standing beside the green, to give perspective to the shot. A useful way of confirming in your own mind that you have correctly judged the distance of a second shot to the green is to imagine that you are, in fact, playing a par-three hole. This can quite often give you a real surprise. By taking a look at the problem from another angle, as it were, you will most times feel that you had under-estimated the shot in the first instance.

In watching amateur golfers I see so many good shots wasted, shots which cover the pin all the way but finish 20 yards short of the green. It is a tragedy for a handicap player to hit his best shot and fail to make par because he has so badly misread the distance he must cover or the distance of which he is capable of hitting the ball. Getting these two factors right can make a vital difference to your scoring.

The technique for shorter shots is basically the same as for the rest of the game, except that the stance becomes narrower and slightly open. I like to move the position of the ball back slightly for the shorter shorts. As we move into the shorter shots and the ball moves closer to the feet, I allow my right foot to move in towards the left and also to move slightly forward, effectively opening the stance. What you should avoid is the old-fashioned idea of getting the ball back opposite the right foot. This requires too many adjustments to make an ordinary shot and makes the game complicated.

As with all shots I feel that the left side must stay in control throughout the swing, but the balance of which we have spoken earlier is imperative— this time the balance between the guiding force of the left arm and side and the very necessary release of the clubhead through the ball with the right and left hands working together. In order to help create an accelerating clubhead in shots which don't require full power it is useful to think of getting the clubhead moving at its fastest beyond the point of impact. By aiming to accelerate the clubhead to a point six inches past the ball you will ensure that you keep the clubhead moving through impact. One more thing to remember—the medium and short irons are designed with sufficient loft to get the ball in the air. They don't need any help from you. Hit down and through with a nice crisp action and the ball will fly. Lean back off the ball and try to scoop it into the air and you destroy the whole concept of medium and short iron play.

With the medium and short irons you should never feel that you are straining for distance. If you have any doubts, take one more club. The essential ingredients of this aspect of the game are rhythm and control.

As we have already discovered that the left side is the controlling side and the right supplies the power, we must ensure that the left side stays in command throughout the swing with the medium and short irons. Although the shots do not demand power as the driver and longer clubs do, they still require acceleration throughout the downswing

From a slightly open stance for the shorter shots, the left arm and side guides the club back to the top of the swing and leads the way back into impact. With this correct amount of control from the left side the hands can then be allowed to release the clubhead into the ball. Without this release the impact will be sluggish and there will be a tendency to steer the ball towards the target, usually with disastrous results.

Rhythm and balance play just as important a part here as they do with the driver. Watch out particularly for those shots which do not require a full swing. It is absolutely essential to maintain your rhythm with the shorter swing. It is very easy to quicken the pace of the swing when the club does not go all the way back. You need a mental metronome to help retain

LEFT SIDE GUIDES

rhythm and crispness with the shorter shots. It can often be very helpful to have a mental key to help retain rhythm such as repeating a key phrase to yourself as you swing. The phrase should match the action, fairly slow and deliberate in the backswing and sharp at impact. If you are concentrating on placing the club in position at the top of the backswing, almost pausing to complete the change from backswing to downswing, and then accelerating firmly into the ball, you might use the key words 'place and hit'.

It is worth spending some time on the practice tee with the shorter clubs because until you have built some confidence in your ability to release the hands into impact and hit the ball where you intend, there will remain that nagging doubt which will tighten up your hand action as you try to place the ball on target. Any attempt to steer the ball with the hands can lead to all sorts of problems. Have confidence in your set-up and your swing and let the ball fly.

Pitching and chipping

With every shot of this kind aim to land the ball on a specific target area of the green or its fringe. It is imperative for any constant success to carefully examine the character of the target, and its relationship to your position.

The average club golfer could save four or five shots in each round of golf by mastering the art of pitching and chipping. It is a department of the game where any player can develop his ability, regardless of age or size.

This is a department of the game where club golfers have every chance of matching the professionals. The swing is short enough to be under complete control and no power is required. Yet as often as a tournament professional will get down in two from just off the green, the amateur will take three or more. I believe it is just as often a lack of clear thinking about what the shot is trying to achieve as any failure of technique which causes the problems. This points up the biggest difference between amateurs and professionals. With every shot of this kind the professional will be aiming to land the ball on a specific target area of the green or the fringe around it. That target will probably be a square yard of turf for a 40-50 yard shot and a smaller area for shorter shots. But the important thing is that the target area will have been carefully worked out in relation to the hole and the slope of the green.

The target area
On the other hand many amateurs play the shot with not much more than a vague idea that the slope comes from the right and they have no specific target in mind. This is imperative for any success with pitching and chipping and we ought to start by examining how that particular target area is established. The starting point must always be the hole and from there two factors come into play—the slope of the green and the trajectory of the shot you must play. The combination of these factors will finally determine your landing point for the ball.

As a general principle you should aim to land the ball on the nearest point of the green, allowing it to run the rest of the way to the hole. The lower, running trajectory of the chip shot is easier to execute and control and therefore the safer type of shot, but this can only be determined by the relative positions of the ball and the hole. Obviously a chip shot cannot be played where there is a bunker between you and the hole or when you are playing sharply uphill. Each situation will dictate its own solution—but the golden rule is to use the simplest method to achieve the correct result.

Sharpen your short game
These are the little shots you can practice in the garden or even the garage. If you are particularly proud of your lawn you can practice very efficiently by hitting shots off a door mat or an old piece of carpet. It certainly saves the grass and gives the right sort of effect. It also makes it possible to practice in the garage during the winter or bad summer weather.

What you should be seeking is a constant speed of impact from a given length of backswing. It is immaterial with this type of practice where the ball finishes as long as you can make it land regularly on the same spot. You must aim at developing a method of hitting your selected target area time after time. For the purposes of garden practice a plastic bucket or cardboard box is all that you need—anything in fact, to form a definite target. On the practice ground you can form a square with four golf clubs. Once you have become reasonably proficient at hitting your target, but not before, then you should try playing to a proper target on the practice putting green, posing yourself as many problems as possible by moving around the green to play long and short shots from uphill and downhill lies. Bring in as much variety as you can—and practice with a friend to bring in an element of competition. A form of clock golf is excellent practice, moving round the green to the positions on the clock face and playing shots from one o'clock, two o'clock and so on. This type of challenge match can do a lot to sharpen up your short game.

Combining strokes

The simplest image to demonstrate exactly what the chip shot should be is to think of it as putting in the air. Every short chip shot is in essence a combination of a putt and a full stroke. You should read the line of a chip shot like a putt but with the ball travelling part of the way in the air. You should be able to exercise the same feeling of control with a short chip as you do with a long putt. In fact, it is often a good idea to use your putting grip for the short chip shots. But don't lose sight of the fact that a chip shot is a different technique and that the hands should be in front of the ball when chipping. Again it is a question of setting the right pattern at address to be repeated at impact. The stance should be narrow and slightly open so that you can look more squarely at the target and have no restrictions in the arm movement through the ball. The angle between left arm and club shaft, which is set at address by ensuring that the hands are in front of the ball, should be retained throughout the chip shot. It is very much an arm swing, maintaining the body position almost as rigidly as with putting, but allowing just sufficient suppleness in the knees to keep balance with the arm movement and promote that all-important rhythm.

There should be just a hint of weight transference to the outside of the left foot, although more than half of the weight remains on the left foot throughout the chipping stroke so that you have the feeling of leading with the left side. Longer chip shots require only a longer backswing and a corresponding increase in the foot and knee movement.

The pitch shot

The pitch is a very different type of shot, designed to get the ball quickly into the air and to stop it effectively by a combination of high, soft trajectory and backspin. This can only be achieved by dealing the ball a sharp, downward blow with the clubhead. Because you want to get the ball up quickly you should use only your most lofted clubs, the pitching wedge or sand wedge to play a 40–50 pitch shot. Always pick the right club for the job. The shot is again played from a narrow, open stance, but this time you can allow the normal action of the hands until the moment of impact when you need to hang on with the left hand, keeping the back of the left hand going towards the target. The right hand must not be permitted to pass the left in the pitch shot swing. Try to get the feeling that the back of the left hand and the palm of the right are pushing the ball towards the hole. It is the one shot where

The shortest, simplest chip shot can best be described as putting in the air. The line and length should be judged as you would judge a long putt and you should have the same feel of control as you would with a putter. Two essential differences are that the hands should be ahead of the ball at address and at impact and there should be just enough flex and movement in the knees to retain balance with the arm movement.

Unfortunately there are no hard and fast rules which say that a 30-inch backswing with a six-iron equals a 30-foot chip shot. It is up to each player to practise chipping with a variety of clubs until he has the feel for length and trajectory which can be achieved from the five-iron to the wedge.

The right length of backswing is essential if you are to achieve accurate chipping. If the backswing is too long for the shot to be played there will be an automatic tendency to slow the club down as it approaches the ball. This is the decelerating swing which we have discussed before and which stands out like a sore thumb in the short game. It leads to a sloppy, fluffed shot which does not get halfway to the hole.

If the backswing is too short you will not be able to get enough acceleration without destroying your swing rhythm. The resultant quick, stabbing chip shot is all too familiar, either hitting the ball on the top and moving it only a few feet or thinning it right across the green. Even the shortest of chip shots must be hit with an accelerating clubhead in order to achieve a firm impact and even the shortest chip shot must also be hit with your own particular swing rhythm.

The fact that the clubhead may only be moving back 18 inches or two feet does not mean that you can afford to ignore the rhythm and timing you have been striving for in the longer shots. Above all these shots should not be hurried. Make sure that you complete the backswing you consider necessary to get the ball to the hole. Feel almost that there is a pause at the end of the backswing before you start the clubhead back towards the ball.

It is by retaining your constant swing rhythm that you will eventually be able to judge the length of these shots by the length of the backswing. Without a regular rhythm there is no way of telling how far the ball will travel even though you hit 20 shots with precisely the same length of backswing.

In your practice session concentrate on retaining your rhythm and landing the ball on a specific target every time. Place two clubs a yard apart on the practice area and try to pitch the ball between them with a variety of clubs from various distances. Regular ten-minute sessions will quickly give you the feel of these shots — and that is the vital ingredient.

THE CHIP

The chip shot is essentially a swing of the arms beneath a firm head position with very little action from the hands and little body movement. It is very similar to the action for a long putt, but at address the hands should be placed ahead of the ball, not level. The other main differences are that the weight should be placed more on the left side for the chip shot, rather than evenly balanced when putting, and there will be a slight movement of the weight to the left at impact, whereas in putting the weight stays evenly distributed between both feet throughout the action.

The stance for the chip shot should be narrow, with the feet very close together. It should also be slightly open, the left foot pulled back a fraction from a line running past the toes to the target. This open stance serves two specific purposes. Firstly it enables you to look more squarely at the target in lining up the shot and secondly it clears the way for the arms to be swung through the ball. A completely square set-up tends to restrict the arm movement through the ball while keeping the clubface aimed at the target.

The knees should be slightly flexed and the weight concentrated more towards the left side, where it will remain throughout the shot. The hands will be ahead of the ball, once again setting up the position at address which you must repeat at impact. The reason the hands are set ahead of the ball is that we want to make contact just before the swing reaches the bottom of its arc. This nips the ball into the air with a degree of backspin which gives more control. If the hands were level with the ball at address and at impact this would

THE PITCH

encourage a scooping action which we have seen is such a bad feature of short iron play.

We have already established the necessity of judging these shots by the length of the backswing and this is why there should be virtually no hand action. A little more action from the right hand into impact will move the ball further than normal from a known length of backswing. By keeping hand action to an absolute minimum, just enough to add some feel to the shot, you will be able to obtain consistent lengths of shot from a known length of backswing while using the same club.

The shot is played entirely with the left side. With the weight largely on the left foot the left arm takes the club back and moves it down and through the ball with the back of the left hand facing the hole throughout the swing. Through the ball the weight will shift slightly further to the left to give the right degree of feel and balance. The knees should remain flexed throughout the swing and the weight should roll easily to the outside of the left foot as the left hand leads the clubface squarely through the ball.

91

THE PITCH

Whereas the chip shot is designed to fly the ball only a short distance through the air and allow it to roll most of the way to the pin, the pitch shot is the reverse. It throws the ball high and stops it quickly. Quite obviously you will need to use your most lofted clubs to achieve this type of shot and ideally they should be played with the wedge or sand wedge. These shots are necessary when faced with a large sand trap between you and the pin or even when the ground between the ball and the green is uneven or particularly wet or dry. Any ground conditions which will not give a normal, even bounce should be avoided. It is much safer to land the ball on the green than to drop it short and hope that it will run straight.

There are two elements within the correctly played pitch shot which will stop the ball quickly. Because the ball gets quickly into the air it has a high, lobbing trajectory. As it drops onto the green, therefore, it does not have a great deal of forward momentum. The most important factor as always, is backspin and as we discovered in dealing with the shots to the green this can only be achieved by hitting down crisply and firmly through the ball. This is the objective of pitch shots.

The set-up for the pitch is the same as for chip shots. The stance is narrow and open and the hands are placed ahead of the ball. Again the weight is slightly to the left of centre at address. The left side is in control all the way, with the left arm taking the club into the backswing. This is where the chip and pitch shots differ. Because we need height and bite on the pitch shots, we must have good hand action. So there is a good wrist break in the backswing, but the right hand must never be allowed to take over. As the left arm guides the club back to

the ball in the downswing, the right hand can be coming into play in the normal way. It is vital that the right hand does not pass the left beyond impact. As with the chip shot, the back of the left hand must face the target well past impact.

Hold on firmly with the left hand and pull it through towards the target, letting the action of the right hand get the clubhead down and through the ball, but not allowing it to destroy the control and accuracy which are vital in these short shots.

The only way to obtain maximum backspin control is with a controlled balance between the guiding role of the left side and the firm impact of the right. Throughout the shot the knees must remain flexed and the body weight will move to the left, rolling to the outside of the left foot. This weight shift and knee flexibility promotes a smooth even rhythm and balance throughout the swing.

You will see at the end of the pitch shot sequence on the left that I have relaxed the hand position at about waist height for a shot of some 45 yards. Yet in the last drawing on the previous page you will see that I am holding the back of the left hand towards the target, not letting the right hand cross over.

On the right I show an over-emphasised form of the left hand position that is so vital to get these pitch shots flying with maximum backspin. Compare this with the drawing showing completely the wrong hand action, with the back of the left hand aiming left and the right hand crossing over.

I think of the pitch shot as a swing without a hit, because at the last moment you do not permit the right hand to come fully into the shot. To get the correct feel of this shot you should exaggerate the left hand position during your practice sessions.

Try hitting wedge shots both ways. First let the right hand come through in the normal way and then try hanging on firmly with the left hand, almost feeling that you are placing the ball on target with the back of the left hand and the palm of the right. I am sure you will notice a significant improvement in your control of these shots. Once you achieve more control you will have more confidence in your ability to hit the correct distance and once your confidence begins to build, you will find you are hitting the shots more firmly and achieving more backspin.

NO CROSS-OVER

correct

incorrect

you are effectively steering the ball into position, unlike the medium and short iron shots where this produces poor results. Because the pitch shot is a short, specialised shot it can be played in this way. I always think of the pitch shot as a swing without a hit.

Short game headaches
Neither the pitch nor chip shot requires a full action and this places a new and vital importance on the length of the backswing. This now becomes your means of adjusting the length of the shot. It needs repeating here that every golf shot must be hit with an accelerating clubhead and in order to achieve this and retain control, at the same time, of the ultimate length of the shot, the length of the backswing has to be directly related to the length of shot. It is a problem which causes more headaches in the short game than any other factor—and it is something which can really be overcome only through practice and experience. Yet this can be achieved quite painlessly once the underlying reasons are understood. Accelerating the clubhead for a full shot causes no problems. You can really release it into the ball and if it flies too far you can adjust by using the same full swing with a shorter club. Yet the very essence of pitching and chipping is to hit the ball the correct distance. This means matching clubhead acceleration to length of backswing. Obviously the very shortest chip from the fringe of the green requires very little acceleration and a short backswing. A pitch shot from 40 yards will require a half swing and considerably more acceleration. By maintaining the constant rhythm which we have been

trying to build into all our golf shots we can make a constant factor of the relationship between backswing length and acceleration. This simplifies the situation enormously because you have only to think of one thing, not two.

Yet, in its turn, this puts more pressure on finding the correct backswing length for each shot. What you will often see—and often have done yourselves, I am sure—is a backswing length totally wrong for the shot to be played. This can take two forms. If the backswing is far too long for the planned shot, the correction must be to slow down the clubhead as it approaches the ball. You will all be familiar with the fluffed, half-missed shot which barely reaches the putting surface and finishes yards from the hole as a result. At the other end of the scale is the back swing which is too short. From this position you cannot smoothly accelerate the clubhead sufficiently to move the ball fast enough while retaining your swing rhythm. The result? Inevitably a quick stab with the clubhead which either stuns the ball dead or sends it shooting across the green. At least you get the chance to practice your chip shot again, but not under the circumstances you would choose.

Directional aids
Once again the key to the whole situation is rhythm. If you can establish a constant rhythm throughout your golf game and apply it strictly to the little shots it becomes so much easier to relate backswing length to shot length. If your rhythm is not constant there is no way that a constant relationship can be established. Hopefully you

SHORT GAME JUDGEMENT

Many factors will influence your decision First, is there any obstruction between you and the hole – a bunker, a lake, a bush or some long grass or uneven ground? Second, where is the hole in relation to your position – on the far side of the green allowing room for the ball to be run up or close to the obstruction you must clear? Third, the lie of the ball – is it a very tight, bare lie, making a pitch shot more difficult, or is there a tuft of grass behind of or in front of the ball? Whatever the problems you should ideally be aiming to land the ball somewhere on the putting surface so that you can be reasonably sure of the type of bounce and roll you can expect.

In the examples shown here, from the back of the green you would have little choice but to throw the ball up quickly over the bank. This would call for a firm, little pitch shot, ensuring that the back of the left hand was pulled through towards the hole. From the right of the green you would have the simplest of short chip shots, with the ball travelling a very short distance in the air and being allowed to roll up to the hole. Rhythm is vital here, with such a short backswing it is very easy to rush the shot. From the front of the green, although you would not have to negotiate the corner of the trap, there is still quite a distance to carry before the ball can land on the green. This calls for a pitch shot because there is not much room between the front of the green and the hole. At the left of the green you would be faced with a long chip shot with plenty of room across the width of the green. You

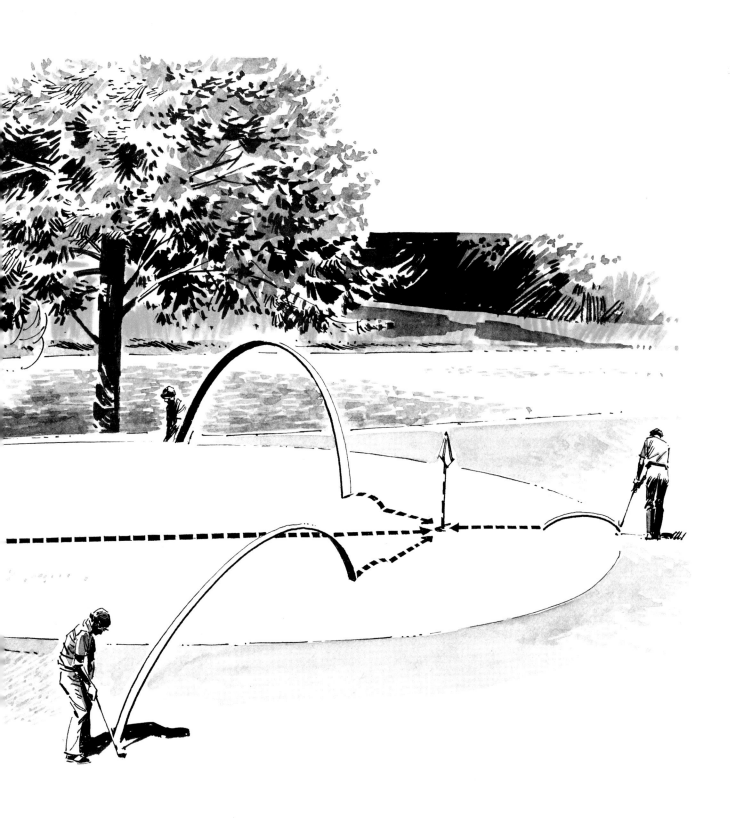

will need a little practice to enable you to judge the amount of roll correctly.

An ideal way to perfect these shots is to get yourself an ever-changing series of tests by playing two or three shots from many positions around the practice putting green. Make the practice competitive by playing against a friend and you will be surprised at how much fun practice can be. Don't be afraid to experiment and to make up shots. If, from the back of the green, for instance, the player found that thick grass behind the ball prevented him playing a normal pitch shot over the bank, he might decide to hit down on the ball with the hands well ahead, bouncing the ball forward into the bank and letting it roll over the top. Or if the pin was much closer to him he could play a cut-up shot, which effectively is a bunker shot played from grass, with the face of the club open and sliding under the ball with an out-to-in action. This will pop the ball into the air very quickly. Once you get the feel of the little shots don't be afraid to try something different. Learning the technique of playing the chip and pitch shots is only part of the battle to improve your scoring. The second and equally important part lies in putting your new found skills to good use. Each short shot around the green needs as much careful planning and thought as you would devote to a long putt. In general terms a running chip shot is safer and easier to play than a high flying pitch shot. Wherever possible you should play the easier of the two, although of course there are many occasions when the pitch shot is the only answer.

have already gone much of the way towards building your overall swing rhythm. Practice of the little shots around the green is also an aid in this direction—in fact it is often recommended as a starting point for aquiring rhythm.

I suggest that you start with the very shortest chip shots, trying to regard them as nothing more than long putts, and gradually move to longer shots. You must also play the same shot with a variety of clubs from the wedge to the six-iron so that you can see the different ways in which the ball will behave, how it will fly higher and roll less with the more lofted clubs. This is all useful knowledge to be applied later on the golf course. I am very much against people having a favourite club for chipping for there is no way that one club can successfully do the job in a variety of situations. On the other hand, if you do use one club particularly well, it is worth building your ability, and above all your confidence, with this club before going on to more extended practice with the full range of clubs.

Above all you are trying to establish a feel for the short game. There is no mathematical formula which says that a 30-inch backswing with an eight-iron will chip the ball 30 feet. There are far too many outside factors involved—and each golfer has a different make-up and swings the club at a different speed. What you will find is that your own built-in computer will very quickly relate the length of *your* backswing to the shot *you* want to play. But as with every computer, it is only as good as the information fed into it. Practice and experimentation are necessary—not for hours on end, but in short interesting sessions— to programme your computer correctly.

Anyone who picks up a golf club has the potential ability to play the little shots well. They don't require power or athletic ability—they do require thought and practice. By using the right technique and with correct application everyone should be able to develop their short game prowess to the point where they get the ball within possible one-putt range six times out of 10 from 30 yards and under.

The potential for improvement and shot-saving is almost certainly greater in the short game than in any other aspect of golf, yet strangely enough this does not seem to be recognised by the higher handicap players. Almost invariably those who can be seen chipping onto the practice putting green are low handicap golfers. Perhaps it is their longer experience in the game that has shown them the benefits to be gained from this type of practice—and perhaps it is the potential embarassment for the poorer players of practising, almost always in front of the clubhouse windows, which puts them off. They should take comfort from the fact that their initial work can be carried out on any corner of the practice ground. The priority is to be able to pitch the ball on a given target and this can be achieved by making a square with four clubs and attempting to land the ball in that area. Once you have developed the ability to land the ball on a given target with a variety of clubs you are well on the way to eliminating wasted shots around the green.

Once you have decided which type of shot you must hit in order to get the ball close to the hole, you must then work back from the hole to pinpoint a target on which to land the ball. If you are chipping this will normally be a spot quite close to the edge of the green, while with a pitch shot it will be a target area closer to the hole. The firmness, speed and contours of the green must all be taken into account in working back to the target area where you must drop the ball.

Having selected this spot I would recommend that you take a couple of practice swings while looking at the hole rather than at the head of the club. This will help you

gauge the distance you must cover for the overall shot. Then take another couple of swings while looking at the spot on which you want the ball to land. These two targets will help your mind and your muscles work out the right length of backswing for the shot to be played. I believe you will find it much easier to judge distance if you follow this procedure.

Let me make a plea here for faster play. If you are going to study these short shots as I suggest, it does not mean that you have to hold up play for the other members of your group. Get on with it while they are looking over their shots or walking to the ball. Good, careful preparation need not take

a long time – most of your decisions can be made as you walk up to the ball. You will certainly be able to see quite clearly how far you are from the green and the position of the pin. The general contours of the green will be obvious. So a quick look at the break you can expect once your ball is rolling on the green and three or four quickly executed practice swings and you should be ready to play as soon as it is your turn. In a group of four golfers, three of them can be working out their shots and getting ready for action while the fourth is playing. Always try to be ready as soon as it is your turn to play.

On the practice area you will find it useful to hit short chip and pitch shots

at a definite target. When it is not convenient to practice on the putting green so that you can judge not only the flight but the roll of the ball, you can practice dropping the ball on a specific target without worrying about where it would roll. This can be done by aiming at a couple of clubs or at your practice ball bag. See how many times you can hit the target with ten shots and then try to improve with every session. Gary Player used to practice bunker shots until he had holed a certain number – a total which he was always increasing. I don't suggest that you have to be this dedicated, but it is useful to monitor your progress in this way.

The art of putting

Putting is golf in a miniature form, it has the same
problems and demands the same basic movements.
You must concentrate on developing a repeating
stroke, striking the ball with the same solid action
every time.

Putting has often been described as a game within
a game, but as far as I am concerned it is merely
golf in miniature. It poses the same problems and
demands the same basic principles. I know you
see a wide range of styles on the putting green, but
the players who are consistently good putters
have three things in common. They operate from
a stance which is basically square and well
balanced; their heads remain almost completely
still throughout the swing; and the face of the
putter repeats its square contact with the ball
every time. It doesn't matter how odd some of the
putting styles may look, you can guarantee that if
they are successful they will incorporate these
three factors. So should your putting action.

The most popular method on tour is without
doubt the pendulum swing, with the triangle
formed by the arms and the shoulders pivoting in
one piece from a point at the base of the neck.
The great benefit of this putting style above most
of the others is that there are so few moving parts
that it really is difficult for things to go wrong once
you have got used to the action. There are very
few areas where error can creep in. Bob Charles is
the best example of the pendulum putting style
you could wish to see.

The wrist action
The relationship between the hands and the
putter face is completely stable because the wrists
do not hinge at all in this action for the shorter
putts. The hands are not involved at all, other
than to form a firm, unmoving link with the club.
This immediately eliminates one of the greatest
areas of uncertainty in putting.

Looking back through the history of the game

there were certainly players of great ability and
feel who putted with a very wristy action. On their
good days they were fantastic, but when things
were not going too well, when that feeling of easy
relaxation was not quite there, they were very
poor indeed. Eliminating the uncertainty of hand
and wrist action from the stroke has not created
players who are significantly better on their good
days, but they are way out in front, still excellent
putters, when their game is less than 100 percent.
It is this type of consistency which is such an
important factor in winning at golf. Cutting out
the frills and fancy work is so often the answer.

The pendulum swing
By blanking off any over-use of the hands in
putting it is quite clear that the putter face works in
unison with the forearms. In the ideal pendulum
swing the arms do not operate independently
either, but are controlled by the shoulders, which
tilt and pivot around the base of the neck.
However, it is here that you can adjust matters to
suit your own particular preference of style. The
important thing is that the arms cannot move
quickly and in an uncoordinated fashion in the
same way as the hands. You are therefore
guaranteeing a better rhythm and consistency.

Use of the pendulum swing also keeps the
putter face on line to the target for a far greater
length of time than any other method, an
invaluable aid in hitting the ball accurately
towards the hole. But you must realise that only
on short putts does the clubhead move straight
back and straight through. It is physically impossible to hold the clubface aimed at the hole
after a backswing of much more than a foot

You will see a larger
variety of styles on the
putting green than
anywhere else—yet good
putters all respect the
basic elements which go
towards a sound repeating
stroke. By far the most
popular method among
tournament professionals
is the firm-wristed
pendulum action.

101

without lifting the head of the putter well off the putting surface. Because all golf swings, including putts, must pivot around the head and spine, the clubhead must always move inside the ball-target line on the backswing. The cardinal error to be avoided in putting is moving the clubhead outside that line—a fault many people fall into by concentrating too hard on moving the clubhead straight back. You can practice this quite easily and see the results extremely clearly by placing a club or a couple of books or magazines three inches beyond the ball, paralleling the line through the ball to the hole. As the clubhead moves back it should be level with your check line for perhaps nine to 12 inches, but will then move away from that line in a gentle curve. This is the natural and correct putting swing line. It is a mistake to force yourself to use anything different.

A sound method

If you are a bad putter the bulk of your initial practice should concentrate on developing a repeating stroke, striking the ball with the same solid action every time. It is only then that you can put the finishing touches of reading the correct line and properly judging pace. Without a repeating stroke and a consistent contact with the ball it is impossible to improve your putting because the ball will react differently to the varying impact implanted on it by your inconsistent stroke. Only when you hit the ball the same way every time can you start to make the minor adjustments which will allow you to develop into a good, regular competitor on the greens. Establish a sound method and stick with it.

Putting is the department of the game where the mental and physical aspects are most obviously linked. You must, clearly, have the right mental approach to hit a vital drive into the correct part of the fairway in the closing stages of a round. Yet if it is less than perfect you still have a chance to recover with your next shot. On the putting green there are no second chances. It is the finite part of the game, with a five-foot putt meaning as much as a 260-yard drive. All the problems are condensed in putting. They are there right in front of your eyes and the mental pressure can build to such an extent that it is difficult to make a smooth stroke at the ball. This is where your practice at making a repeating stroke will be invaluable and also where your subconscious golfing rhythm will play its part. There is as much rhythm involved in a successful putting action as in a full-blooded drive.

Many players find that total concentration is the most difficult part of putting. Certainly you will not putt well unless you can bring full concentration to bear on what you are doing. We will deal later with the various ways of assessing putts, but once you have decided on the correct line you should then look between the ball and the hole while you take one or two practice swings and try to picture the exact line along which the ball will roll to the hole. With this line clearly in your mind and a last look at the hole to confirm the distance you are now ready to make your stroke. Stare at a spot on the back of the ball where the putter will

The pendulum putting style is the most widely used and successful in the world of tournament golf. The underlying answer is not hard to find. The method gets its name from the backwards and forwards movement of a clock pendulum and, when practiced correctly, there is just about as little to go wrong.

The triangle formed by the arms and shoulders pivots in one piece from a point at the base of the neck. The hands play no active part at all, merely forming a firm link between the arms and the putter. There are so few moving parts that it is difficult for things to go wrong once you have got used to the method.

If you are already a good putter you will probably do well to stick with whatever method is working for you, but anyone who needs to improve on the greens will be well advised to try the system which so many professionals use successfully.

You will see a large variety of styles at your own club and on the tournament circuit, but just as there are many idiosyncrasies in the full swings of many players which still incorporate the basic fundamentals, the same is true in putting. Good putters will always strike the ball squarely, consistently and repetitively. They will do so from a generally square set-up which is solid and well-balanced, the head virtually unmoving throughout the stroke. Any putting action which incorporates these three points has very real chances of being successful.

The area where most errors creep into the putting stroke is the action of the hands. If the wrists hinge allowing hands to play an active part in the stroke, it becomes more and more difficult to make the action repeat time after time. The important factor about the

pendulum method is that the hands do not move at all, allowing the rhythm, the pace and the strength of the putting stroke to be dictated by the forearms. In this way it is much easier to build a repeating stroke, which is the essence of all good putting.

It has been noticeable over the years that players who employ a

wristy action in their putting stroke tend to be inconsistent, sometimes brilliant, but often well below average. Elimination of the wristy stroke by use of the pendulum method has largely done away with this inconsistency, the modern tournament player being a steadily good performer on the greens.

Even with the pendulum method you must realise that the clubhead cannot move straight back and straight through for anything but short putts.

Because the pendulum swing pivot about a point at the base of the neck it must move the putter inside the line through the ball to the hole, just as any full shot does. As with the full shots, the worst mistake you can make is to take the putter back outside this line. You can check your own action easily by placing two clubs on the lounge carpet about six inches apart and then place your putter between them and try putts of varying length. It very quickly becomes clear that on longer putts the club moves inside the line. At the same time any tendency to take the club outside the line can be spotted and cured.

THE PENDULUM STROKE

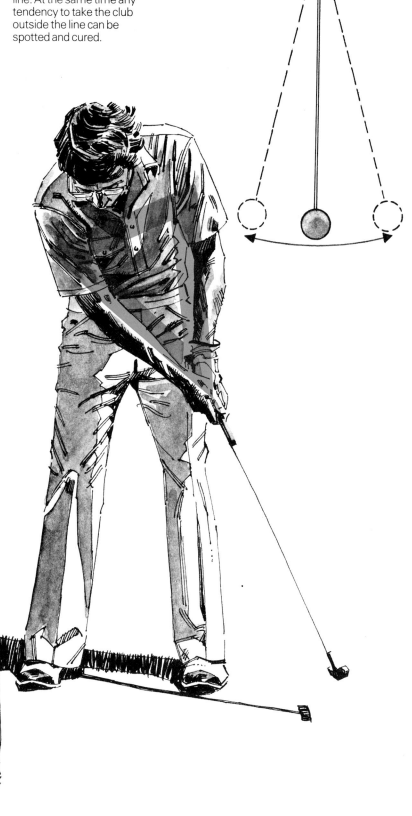

It is not always easy to judge whether your eyes are above the ball-target line, but there is a simple way to test your own putting set-up at home. Take up your normal putting position and, without moving the body or putter positions, take your right hand off the club and take a small coin from your pocket. Keeping as still as possible, hold the coin beside your right eye and then drop it. This will illustrate very clearly whether you have achieved the ideal putting posture. Very seldom will the coin fall beyond the ball, as most golfers set themselves up in a position where the eyes will be directly above a point between the ball and the feet. If this is the case you should adjust your posture and ball position until the eyes are above the ball. It will undoubtedly feel uncomfortable to start with, but with a little practice on the lounge carpet you will soon be able to adopt this position naturally. I am sure you will find it considerably easier to aim the putter face at the hole in this way.

Another important factor in the putting set-up is the position of the ball laterally in relation to the feet. I don't feel that a good putting stroke can be perfected if the ball is further back than the midway point between the feet. Any ball position to the right of the centre point between the feet will lead to a downward movement of the putter head as it strikes the ball because you will be making contact before the lowest point of the swing arc. This will squeeze the ball slightly into the turf and make it jump, giving a far from consistent result.

It is worth reminding ourselves what the putting stroke is trying to achieve. From a well-balanced and firm basis the upper body should be angled forward far enough to allow free movement of the arms from the shoulders; the eyes should be over the ball; and the ball should be in the forward half of the stance so that the putter blade can roll it forward with no downward blow. Putting is the precision part of golf, where the smallest error in judgement of line or length or the slightest flaw in technique can

mean a dropped shot – or worse. Because accuracy is the all-important factor in putting, and power plays no part at all, we can adjust the normal set-up position to give ourselves the best possible chance of aiming correctly.

Unlike the longer shots, where it is a positive disadvantage to lean too far forward from the waist, your putting stance should place your eyes directly over the line through the ball to the hole. When firing a rifle you don't hold the gun away from the side of your body and point it in the general direction of the target, you get your eye directly behind the sight and look along that sight line at the target. Exactly the same principle applies in putting. By having your eyes directly above the ball you can aim the face of the putter at the hole with much more precision than if you were standing more upright with the ball perhaps a foot in front of you.

EYES OVER THE BALL

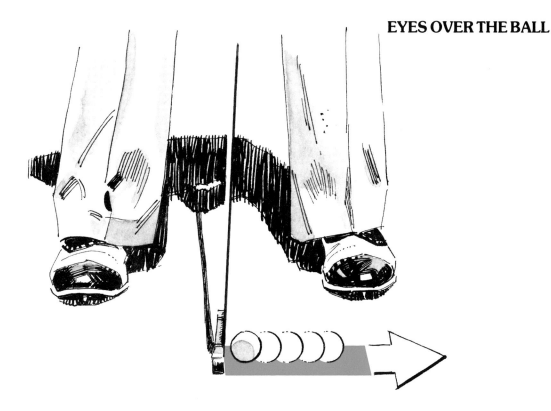

As with every other golf shot, perfect putting is an exact combination of correct line and length. With short putts the distance is not difficult to judge and therefore most of the concentration must be towards determining the correct line, but with longer putts the general line becomes more obvious and the critical factor becomes the judgement of length.

With very little examination of the line most golfers will be able to get the ball within three feet of either side of the hole from around 30 feet, but very often they will be more than three feet short or past the hole. It can often be helpful to imagine a three-foot radius circle drawn around the hole, for it can be far easier to stop the ball within this larger circle than aiming at the much smaller target of the hole itself.

However, this is only a useful hint in judging distance and does not get down to the root cause for those people who consistently fail to get the ball close to the hole. Before any golfer can become a good putter he must learn to strike the ball the same way every time. As we discovered when discussing chip shots, the length of the backswing has a vital affect on the distance the ball travels, but the relationship between backswing length and length of shot is only relevant when shots are hit consistently with the same rhythm and the same clubhead acceleration.

Only when you are fairly confident that your putting stroke will repeat time and time again, especially under pressure, should you devote time to perfecting your aiming techniques. Combining these two skills will mean that you can confidently roll the ball close to the hole from any distance.

Concentration is often the key to putting and I focus my attention rigidly on a spot on the back of the ball where the putter head will strike. This is after I have selected the line and judged the distance, but now my attention is drawn down to this one point and it allows all my thinking to concentrate on a firm, even stroke. I look at the ball so hard, in fact, that once I have struck the putt I can still see a dark, shadow-like after-image of the ball.

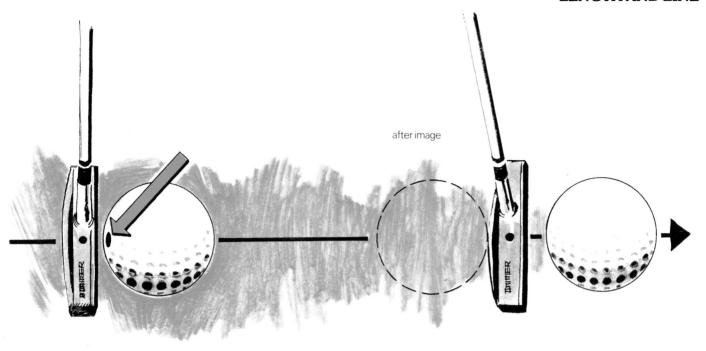

after image

make contact and concentrate on this spot until after you have hit the ball.

Direction and concentration

Personally I look so hard at this point that I see a dark after-image of the ball after I have hit it towards the hole. I believe that if you give yourself something difficult on which to concentrate you will have few problems in that direction. I find that loss of concentration, a sloppy mental attitude, often comes from an unclear idea of what you are trying to achieve. Once you begin to concentrate on the planning details, the essential ingredients of any attempted golf shot, you will become too deeply involved for your mind to wander. As a general rule the most difficult part of putting is the judgement of distance. Most of us can read the line of a putt well enough to get the ball passing within two to three feet of either side of the hole — but how often are you six feet short or five feet past? Only you will know how far you hit the ball with your normal putting stroke — and you will only know this accurately once you have made that stroke repetitive. However, there are one or two useful tips for taking the chance out of this part of the game which you ought to try.

On long putts it is always a good idea to walk between your ball and the hole. I don't think it is necessary to count the number of paces, although you might find it it helpful. But it does plant in your mind the actual distance to be covered—not just your impression of that distance from the foreshortened view from behind the ball. With long putts you should also take a look from the side as well as from behind because even a very slight overall slope going with or against the putt can make perhaps three feet difference at the hole from 30-40 feet. But please carry out these examinations while others are studying their putts—we don't want to create any slower play than we have right now. Be ready to play when it is your turn. There is a popular method of helping line up putts which I believe can be just as useful for helping to judge distance. It is a method used by Jack Nicklaus and many of the other leading tournament players, although I have not found that it helps me particularly.

Never up, never in

When lining up a putt from behind the ball, pick a spot not far in front over which it will run on its way to the hole. This can be anything from a slightly different colour in a small patch of the green to an oddly shaped blade of grass. There is always something if you look hard enough. The idea is that when you stand over the ball you have an aiming point for the line of your putt which you can see quite clearly just in front of the ball. You know that if you roll the ball over that spot it will be on line for the hole. I feel that this idea is of equal value in helping judge distance for the simple reason that the alignment of the putt is taken care of so that in the last few seconds before you strike the ball, virtually all of your concentration can be aimed at striking the ball at the correct speed. Try it and see how it works out.

STUDY THE ANGLES

Having mastered the technique of striking consistent putts, we now come to the art of reading greens correctly so that your solid striking is not wasted by poor application. Right at the start I want to emphasise that you can study putts in detail in your attempts to get the best possible results, but you should on no account slow down the play of your own match and those following Golf at club level has been getting slower and slower over the years as more players go through the routines used by the professionals on tour. Anything which would further slow down play must be eliminated.

A great deal of work can be put into your putting as you approach the green and as your partners putt out. The overall contours of the green will usually show up quite clearly as you approach the putting surface and you can study the exact line from behind your ball as someone else is taking their putt. If you need to take a look from the side or from behind the hole, then move quickly about the green, preferably changing your vantage point between putts taken by your fellow players. Where possible, be ready to putt when it is your turn. If you are first to play, then complete your study without wasting time – and hope that your partners have done their homework while you are going to work on your putt.

On long putts it can often be helpful to walk between your ball and the hole. Some people like to count the number of paces to help them make their judgement, but often

it is enough merely to cover the distance and be sure of it, rather than depending solely on a foreshortened view from behind the ball. Another good idea is to take a sideways view of the putt, standing off to one side of the line from the ball to the hole at about its mid-way point. A few practice swings while looking between the ball and the hole will help you get the feel of the strength of stroke you will need. From this position you will also see if there are any hidden slopes or up down to the hole. You can easily leave the ball well short of the hole or charge it well past if you do not take the trouble to have a sideways look.

If it is a really tricky putt you may feel you should double check your judgement of the line by looking back from the hole to the ball.

Sometimes this can show difficult contours because the light is catching them from a different angle. I check the break of a putt by holding my putter in front of my face with just the thumb and fore-finger and allowing it to hang absolutely perpendicular.

This then acts like the cross hair on a rifle sight, giving you a known, constant factor against which to check the slope of the ground.

To putt well you must be armed with as much information as possible before you stand over the ball – but remember, it shouldn't take you all day.

EVERY PUTT IS STRAIGHT

Two factors effect the speed and break of a putt — the moisture in the green and the grain of the grass. Grain is not really a problem in Britain, where the grass is very fine-bladed, but it can cause problems in America and other parts of the world. Grain is the direction in which the grass grows. As you look down the grain the green will have a light shiny look. Turn round and look in the other direction and the grass will appear to be a darker colour. Putting with the grain will mean that the ball will roll further. If you putt against the grain it will pull up much more

quickly. If the putt breaks from the left and the grain is growing from the right, the grain will largely cancel out the slope of the green. Yet if the putt breaks with the grain you will have to allow for a bigger break than normal.

The amount of moisture in a green can have similar effects. Slow, wet greens will demand a firmer stroke to get the ball to the hole and the ball will break less than normal. Very dry, fast greens, on the other hand, require a much more delicate touch and all the contours will be exaggerated.

On average, a tournament professional

I am sure you have all heard the expression 'never up, never in.' There can be no argument with its message. Any putt which fails to reach the hole is a missed opportunity to improve your score. But this does not mean that charging the ball six feet past the hole is better than being one foot short. Ideally you should hit every putt at a speed which will take it one foot past the hole if you fail to hole it. Even on those rare occasions when you have hit a really bad putt and you can see it is going to miss the hole and finish well past—don't turn away in disgust. Watch the ball carefully. It could save you the embarassment of missing the return. The amount of break the ball takes past the hole is exactly the amount of break you must allow for when trying to hole out. It is a perfect guide to the next putt which many people never see.

Country and climate

Putting varies enormously in different parts of the world and I would say that putting in Britain and Europe is an easier matter than trying to hole out in America. The reason is simply that the fine-bladed grass in Britain and Europe has virtually no grain or nap, while the putting surfaces in America do. When putting in the same direction as the grain the ball will move faster and break more. Against the grain it will be a slower putt with less break. Putting across the grain will increase or reduce the normal effects of any slope. You can spot the direction of growth of the grain by the colour. Looking down the grain the grass will look quite light coloured with a distinct shine. Against the grain it looks much darker. If in any doubt take a look at the hole and you will see the direction in which the grass is growing around the lip. The direction of growth will be quite obvious.

In countries which have no significant grain the amount of break on a putt is controlled only by the slope and the speed of the green. Only through experience will you be able to judge the amount of break dictated by certain slopes, but for most people this comes quite easily and naturally. Two general rules to bear in mind are that wet or slow greens hold the ball more on line, reducing the amount of break, while fast, dry greens mean you should allow for more break than normal. If you have trouble assessing the slope of a green, look at the surrounding terrain. Almost certainly any hidden slopes in the green will fall in the same direction as the slopes of the surrounding area.

Reliance on a sound, repeating stroke has to be the key to good putting. Any method which allows the same firm stroke every time has to be correct for each individual. If the contact between clubhead and ball is not consistent it becomes impossible to judge the distance the ball will travel for any length of backswing. This not only effects distance but the amount the ball will break on the green. Where a firmly struck putt will hold its line across a slope, but must catch the hole squarely because it is travelling faster and may spin off from either side, a less resolute putt will fall off line well short of the hole. If you are unsure of how firmly your action will strike the ball, how do you know which line to take to the hole? Practise at home building up a repeating putting stroke.

will take five or six putts less in a round than most club golfers. This is partly because he will hit approach shots closer to the hole, but also because he will make far fewer putting errors. Sensible work on this aspect of the game could save you two or three shots in every round.

Before every putt Jack Nicklaus picks out a small spot just a few feet in front of the ball which is exactly on the line he wants to roll the ball. This may be a light or dark spot on the grass or even an oddly shaped blade of grass—if you look hard enough you will always

find something. Having studied his putt from all sides and decided on the line, he picks this spot so that he can line up the blade of the putter more easily on a close object than on the distant hole.

Although I do not use this method myself, I feel it can be of tremendous use to many club golfers in helping not only the alignment of their putts, but also in their judgement of distance. If you are confident that you have the putter correctly aimed by lining it up with your close-up aiming point, you will be able to devote more of your concentration to getting

the ball to roll the correct distance. By taking care of one of the putting problems it frees you to use more of your mind on the other.

Another important aspect of putting is that every putt is a straight putt when you hit it. Quite obviously, here I have decided that the right to left slope calls for a break of two feet or so. What it is easy to forget is that as you strike the ball on your chosen line you are hitting a straight putt along that line. I have seen golfers read a break correctly, but then drag the ball round at impact subconsciously steering it to the hole.

Playing from sand traps

Just because you are in the sand don't be intimidated and let your swing rhythm desert you. Sand requires a special shot and for the only time you have to swing out-to-in with an open clubface.

Sand probably causes more problems on the golf course than any other hazard. Yet with the right clubs and application of a much misunderstood technique, golfers of all categories can dispel their fear of this shot and learn to be proficient out of sand.

Getting out of sand is one of the few times in golf that you should be trying to swing the club differently. It is a special shot that calls for an out-to-in swing with the clubface open so that it can slide under the ball. It is a shot which causes untold problems for amateur golfers, mainly because they are frightened to death at the very thought of playing from sand. The first thing to desert them is their swing rhythm and this is fatal. Probably more than in any other area of the game you must maintain rhythm to get any result at all. Let's adopt our normal procedure of examining what the shot is trying to achieve and then assess the technical ways in which this becomes possible.

Look behind the targets at a rifle range and what do you find? That's right—bags full of sand. Sand has the ability to absorb the energy of a bullet so quickly that it will stop it dead within a few feet. It is not surprising that it can kill a badly hit trap shot the way it does. That is why a special technique has to be employed—one which allows the leading edge of the club blade to slice through the sand rather than digging into it. The whole theory of sand shots is based around this fact, although one or two specialised shots requiring a slightly different technique will be dealt with later. Perhaps one of the most graphic ways of demonstrating how the sand shot should work is by proving to yourself the ways in which it most clearly does not work! Try a normal short chip shot out of sand and you will find that unless you pick the ball absolutely cleanly the clubhead will slow down so quickly when it makes contact with the sand that the ball will move almost no distance either in the sand or in the air.

Without using a ball, take a few larger swings using your normal chipping or pitching action and see just how fast the clubhead grinds to a halt as the square face digs into the sand. That's how not to play the shot! Yet so often that is exactly how people try to play it. Now try it the right way—but again without the ball. Take up an open stance, the line across the feet, hips and shoulders pointing well left of the target. The blade of the club should be aimed right of the pin and will therefore appear wide open because you are aiming your whole body well to the left. Hold the club with a real feeling of relaxed flexibility in the hands. This is one shot you can't play with too firm a grip. Relaxed wrists and hands will also allow more feeling for the rhythm of the stroke. The very thing we have been trying to avoid throughout the rest of our golf game—taking the clubhead back outside the line—is exactly what we want to achieve here. In fact, by setting up with the body line aimed well left of the target you assure an outside swing line from the start.

The open clubface
Begin with a half-swing and plenty of easy rhythm and try to have the feeling that you are bouncing the clubhead off the sand—the way you skated flat stones across the lake when you were a kid. Swing the clubhead through to a complete finish. Avoid stabbing at the sand—the clubhead must keep going. Practice this swing several times without a ball, making sure that the clubhead bounces through the sand. Some people like to have the thought that they are almost scraping the sand with their right hand in

SAND SHOTS

Another basic factor of sand play is sound footing. It is very easy for your feet to slide around in sand while taking the full, free swing which is necessary to obtain good results. With every sand shot you must ensure that you twist your feet about until they have sunk sufficiently into the sand to ensure that you have a firm base around which to swing. Obviously the amount that you sink into the sand will vary, depending upon the type of sand and whether it is wet or dry. On some courses the sand is extremely fine and light and you can easily go down three or four inches before you are satisfied with your stance. At other clubs the sand, is heavy and coarse and even with a good deal of waggling you will not get down more than an inch.

Having overcome the problem of a sound base for the swing, you have inadvertently created another problem. You are now between one and four inches closer to the ball than if you were playing the same shot off the turf. You must compensate by moving the hands down the grip by an equivalent amount or you will be digging deep into the sand behind the ball instead of skimming the clubface through the top surface just under the ball.

On the question of how far behind the ball the clubhead should enter the sand, this is really something that you will work out for yourself once you have begun to build confidence with your method. It should be something like one and a half to two inches behind the ball. It will vary with the type and condition of the sand and this is where you can learn a lot when digging your feet in before the shot. The amount of resistance you will feel through your feet will give you a very clear idea of the condition of the sand. Often the sand will look powdery and dry on the surface, but if there has

been a lot of rain earlier it is quite possible that half an inch down the sand may well be very wet and compacted. This will affect the way you play the shot.

In very dry, light sand you can afford to hit further behind the ball because the clubhead will move quite easily under the ball. In heavier, wet sand you must strike the sand much closer to the ball to get the same results.

Having judged the conditions and the shot I wish to play I adopt a similar method of concentration to my putting technique. Instead of picking out a spot on the back of the ball, I pick out an individual grain of sand at the right distance behind the ball and concentrate all my attention on that grain until I hit it with the leading edge of the clubface.

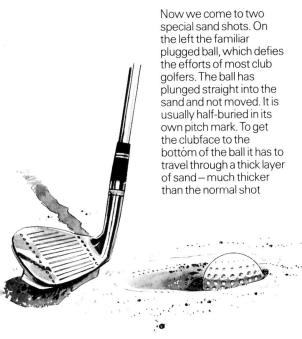

Now we come to two special sand shots. On the left the familiar plugged ball, which defies the efforts of most club golfers. The ball has plunged straight into the sand and not moved. It is usually half-buried in its own pitch mark. To get the clubface to the bottom of the ball it has to travel through a thick layer of sand – much thicker than the normal shot

where the ball is sitting on top of the sand. There is a point beyond which the normal splash-type of sand shot will not be effective. The very nature of this shot, bouncing the clubhead into and through the sand, means that it cannot penetrate very deep and therefore the plugged ball calls for an entirely different shot, one much more allied to your normal game.

In this case the stance should not be as open as before, more like the normal set-up for a pitch shot. The clubface should also revert to normal, the leading edge of the blade being square to the target, not open. This shot calls for a firm downward blow, hitting the sand

much closer to the ball than in the splash out. Often the ball will create a depressed ring around itself as it plugs in the sand. Aim at the edge of this ring. Because you are hitting down and into the sand there will be no follow through, the sand stopping the clubface very quickly on impact. It can take quite a firm shot to move the ball from wet sand.

The result of the shot will be quite different as well. Because you will not have such a lofted clubface at impact the ball will come out lower and faster and will not stop as quickly. You should plan the shot accordingly.

The long bunker shot, below is another useful

addition to your armoury, but it calls for caution and common sense. You must select your club very carefully to ensure that you have enough loft to clear the front of the trap and any banks surrounding it. You must also remember that any contact with the sand before the ball is struck will kill the shot instantly. You must hit the ball first, just as you should with an iron shot from the fairway. To help with this you can move the ball slightly to the right in the stance, encouraging the downward, ball-sand impact. Choke down on the grip because in digging your feet into the sand you will have moved closer to the ball.

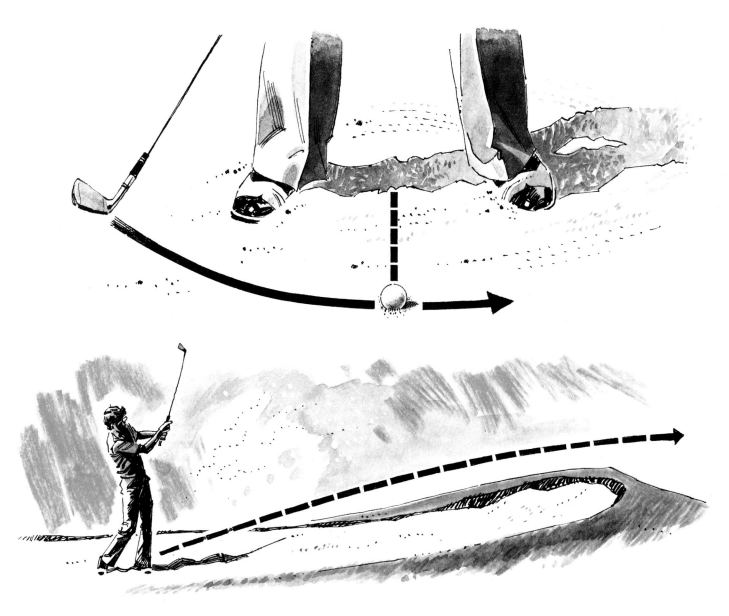

this shot, matching the action of the hand with that of the clubhead in their mental image.

Once you have begun to feel the shot correctly it will be time to try it for real. Keep the same swing pattern and rhythm in your mind and splash the clubhead down as if you are not going to make contact with the ball at all, as if the clubhead is going to pass completely under the ball. One very graphic description I have heard is to imagine that the ball has legs and that the leading edge of the clubhead is going to slice them off as it passes through the sand underneath. Whatever image you use, the facts remain beyond question. The way to hit a normal bunker shot is by sliding an open clubface through the sand. Remember what happens to a bullet when it plunges straight in — it almost stops dead.

A lot is often talked about how far behind the ball you should hit the sand with the clubhead. Personally I like to concentrate so hard on this aspect that I pick an individual grain of sand one-and-a-half to two inches behind the ball and make sure that is where the clubhead strikes. But once you have understood the technique of the shot and are conscious of the need to slide the clubhead under the ball, you will automatically pick your own spot. Once you are able to play the shot the right way, this becomes an almost insignificant detail which will solve itself. Your experience in playing and practicing these shots will teach you the right spot to hit. Yet all the emphasis on hitting the sand at an exact spot is of no use at all if the swing technique is faulty.

The plugged ball

There are two other basic forms of bunker shot which you should learn how to handle because they crop up at regular intervals in any golfer's life and because they require a different approach. Probably the most difficult is the plugged shot, where the ball has landed heavily in the sand and settled well down. In order to get the leading edge of the clubface to the bottom of the ball it has obviously got to get through a thicker layer of sand than with the normal trap shot. There is a point beyond which our normal bounce or splash shot will not be effective, will not be able to penetrate far enough into the sand to achieve the result we seek. The answer is altogether a more normal set-up and a square clubface position at address and at impact. This is a shot where you really do have to dig quite steeply into the sand and a full follow-through, such a hallmark of the normal bunker shot, will not be possible. Often the ball will create a depressed ring in the sand as it plugs itself in. If this is the case you should aim to hit the edge of this ring with the leading edge of the clubface. The shot must be a firm, downward blow, penetrating the sand closer to the ball than in the normal trap shot. The power you use will be dictated by the distance the ball must cover and the condition of the sand. In wet sand it can take quite a strong action to shift the ball.

Remember also that the ball will come out lower and faster than the basic trap shot, and with less backspin. The high trajectory of the normal shot, and its backspin, means that it will settle quite quickly once it has pitched on the green and

The normal recovery shot from sand is the only time in golf you should be trying to swing the club differently. We have seen the results of an out-to-in swing in the long game — almost always a weak, glancing blow and a slice. To get out of sand this is exactly the type of shot we need. It is the only time I can think of where two golfing wrongs make a right.

Because sand is able to absorb energy so rapidly any normal shot with the leading edge of the club digging into the sand would give no results at all. That is why a specially designed club and a special technique are required to allow the leading edge of the blade to slice through the sand.

To encourage an out-to-in swing line, the feet, hips and shoulders should be aimed well left of the target and the clubface pointed to the right of the target. The hands should be very light on the grip of the club, encouraging a quick pick up of the clubhead and plenty of easy rhythm throughout the swing. If the club is picked up quickly on an outside line it will return to the ball from the same. With the clubface open, pointing to the right of the target,

there will be an enormous amount of loft on the clubface and it will slide into the sand under the ball rather than digging in.

The ideal address position for bunker shots has the ball placed towards the heel of the club. This is because the swing is very much from the outide with an open clubface and will mean that the ball will, in fact, be played from the middle of the clubface.

On the right you can clearly see the very open stance when looking back from the hole. Feet, hips and shoulders are aimed very much to the left of the hole and the face of the club is aimed to the right. The line of the swing is shown by the broad, dark arrow, while the thin, I arrow indicates the laid back aspect of the clubface. At the start of the swing you can see how quickly the club has been picked up on the outside line, already a lot of wrist action and the clubface still wide open.

HIGH FINISH

Continuing through the sand shot swing we see that the club is taken back into a fairly full turn on the backswing and that there is plenty of hand action through the ball, with the hands and the club coming right through to a high finish. This finish is vitally important because it shows that there has been no stabbing action into the ball, but a release of the clubhead under and through the ball — the only way to success for the normal sand shot.

There are one or two graphic mental images which can help your bunker play. Remember how you used to skate flat stones across the surface of the lake when you were young? That is a similar action to the successful trap shot. If you can imagine the action of the right hand bouncing the head of the club off the sand then you are beginning to get the right image. Rather than the clubhead digging into the sand to lift the ball out it slides into the sand behind and under the ball, almost with the feeling that the clubhead does not make contact with the ball at all, but that the ball floats out on a cushion of sand. I have even heard people describe the ball as having legs which the leading edge of the clubface slices off as it passes through the sand under the ball.

All these images and the high follow-through will allow the rounded sole of the sand-iron to slide through the sand and keep going. Try a normal chip or pitch shot from sand and you will see how quickly contact with the sand will stop the clubhead.

Far too many club golfers set themselves squarely for shots from sand and try to scoop the ball out with a square clubface. This cannot give good results and so confidence vanishes and with it the swing rhythm. Once you have reached this state you have just about no chance of ever getting out of sand again.

Remember that you cannot ground the club in these circumstances and to prevent any tension building up as you address the ball in the correct open manner, you should shrug the shoulders and waggle the clubhead. This will free you for the full, rhythmic swing which is required.

By using the correct technique you will not automatically get brilliant results at once, but you will get the ball out of the sand and slowly your confidence and ability will grow. You will be building up towards a complete golf game rather than skulking in a department which you know will always let you down.

you can afford to aim it fairly close to the pin. With the plugged shot you will not have that degree of control and should not try to be too ambitious. Getting the ball on the green, or back onto the cut grass from a fairway bunker should be sufficient ambition—to start with at least. And that leads us to the study of fairway bunker shots, where distance, not accuracy, is the prime concern. First you must use good judgement in deciding which club will get the ball into the air quickly enough to clear the lip of the trap or any mounds or shaping around it. If you have any doubt at all you should go to the shorter club. You are far better off hitting an eight-iron into the fairway than catching the lip with a six-iron and being faced with the same shot, or a worse one, all over again.

As we have discovered, unless you are using a sand wedge in the correct manner, any contact between the clubhead and the sand before the ball can be disastrous. With long shots out of bunkers the ball must be hit before the sand, like a normal fairway shot where you hit the ball before

the turf. In order to make this easier you can position the ball further back towards the centre of the stance. This will enable you to hit confidently into the ball without fear of contacting the sand first. On all bunker shots you should settle yourself well into the sand so that you have a firm footing for the swing. There is an added bonus here because it will also give you a clear indication of the texture and condition of the sand. Often sand can look dry and powdery on the surface, yet half-an-inch down it can be quite wet and solid. This valuable information can be learned through the feet. Don't forget to compensate for wriggling your feet down into the sand by going an equal amount down the shaft on the grip. A good many poor bunker shots are played because the golfer has effectively reduced his height and therefore his distance from the ball and has failed to compensate by going down the shaft in the grip in order to reduce the length of the shaft. Confidence and correct technique is the key to good bunker play.

Bad lies and trouble shots

Trouble lurks around every corner on the golf course. It is important to tackle problem shots with a clear head, and an understanding of the techniques involved – all achieved through practice.

Trouble comes in many shapes and forms during a round of golf, from water to deep rough, from sidehill lies to huge trees. You can go most of the way to overcoming them by keeping a cool head and a steady swing rhythm.

Getting out of trouble is an almost everyday occurence in golf. Nobody, not even the greatest professional players in the world, play many rounds which don't involve more than a few problems. They may not be deep in the woods or lost at the bottom of a lake, but they will certainly be off the fairway, will face uphill and downhill lies or have to pitch from a bare lie to a close pin position over a yawning bunker. These are the shots which make up the problems in golf. Those who play consistently well are either those who make very few mistakes, or those who have a very real talent for recovering from difficult spots.

There are two essential requirements for making good recoveries from trouble—a cool head and a steady swing rhythm. First you must analyse the problem sensibly so that you can plan the most expedient way out of trouble and then you must be able to execute that recovery by swinging at your own set rhythm. Another excellent quality for recovery shots is ingenuity, the ability to make shots to fit any situation. You may have to fashion shots out of mixed materials, doing things you have never tried before. A variety of circumstances can have an effect on how you play recovery shots other than the obvious ones imposed by trees, traps and the dozens of other dangers which lurk at every turn on the golf course. If you are playing a medal round you will, quite naturally and properly, be more intent on getting the ball back safely into play by the simplest and most direct route. On the other hand, if it is a match-play situation, you could well throw caution to the winds if you had no chance of making an impression on your opponent by the safe route.

You should examine the problem thoroughly from all angles, decide the safest method of recovery and then look beyond that to see if the particular circumstances of your round will allow you to take a bolder approach. This does not mean that you should take hours over your decision. I am very much against anything that makes play any slower than it has become. You are quite capable of assessing the general situation as you approach your ball. You will know, for instance, that there is a deep bunker between you and the pin, that the wind is blowing strongly from the left and that the bush over which you must play your next shot is at least 15 feet high. You can programme this into your computer as you walk to the ball, adding the details of the lie of the ball and its distance from the bush when you get up close. If you think ahead you can take great care without taking a great amount of everyone's time.

An element of realism
In weighing up the pros and cons of the shot you must play, remember that it is you who has to play the shot. Many people mentally endow themselves with the ability of Arnold Palmer or Severiano Ballesteros and finish up attempting shots over which even these great recovery players would hesitate. Be realistic about your ability and plan accordingly. You quite often find that players of modest normal ability play the difficult shots extremely well. This might be because the unusual demands of the difficult situation force them to concentrate in a manner which they don't apply to their normal game. There is nothing like an impossible situation for

121

sharpening the concentration and making the mind click into top gear.

Before we go into specific techniques for dealing with problem shots there is one overall thought to bear in mind. When you have decided on the type of shot you wish to play, select the club with the right amount of loft to do exactly that job. In general terms you are making the shot more difficult if you use an eight-iron but close the face because you want the ball to fly relatively low. Take the six-iron in the first place and play a normal shot. Although it is impossible to set out a recovery drill for every eventuality you may face on the golf course, there are nine basic shots which you will encounter quite regularly—too regularly you might say.

Down in the rough

Let's start with the most obvious—playing the ball from the rough. The key thought here is to keep the clubhead out of the grass as much as possible. This means that the club should be picked up steeply in the backswing and brought back down sharply into the back of the ball on the downswing. This is the only way you will keep the contact between club and ball as clean as possible. The more grass that gets between the clubhead and the ball the less distance and control you will have over the shot. I know many amateurs think that in playing from rough the blade of the club will be forced open. In fact, from long grass, the opposite is true. The grass seems to cling around the heel of the club, closing the clubface. So in these circumstances it is often wise to aim off slightly to the right. You will need a firm left hand grip for these shots.

Hitting a ball high to clear a tree or to land a ball softly from a steep trajectory on a difficult green you will need to position the ball further forward than for a normal shot, use a light grip and get plenty of hand action going into the ball. Don't scoop at the ball, really get the clubhead moving and let the club loft do the job. At the opposite end of the scale, to keep a ball low under a tree branch or to punch the ball forward into the wind, you will have to place the ball further back in the stance than normal. This will automatically put the hands ahead of the ball in the address position and this is exactly where they should be at impact. Have the feeling of hitting crisply into the ball with a firm-wristed action.

Uphill, downhill and sidehill

Some of the most difficult shots to play well are those uphill, downhill and sidehill lies which at first sight do not look too dangerous. The answer to them all is in the correct positioning of the body at address to allow the club to be swung through the ball as normally as possible. When playing uphill it is important to set the body at right angles to the slope, avoiding the temptation to lean into the hill. If you keep the clubhead low to the ground on the take-away this will encourage you to hit through along the slope after impact when there is usually a tendency to stop the swing abruptly. The same principle applies to playing from a downhill lie. Set the body correctly at address and chase the clubhead down the slope

The first thing you must remember when you get into trouble on the golf course is who you are and what your handicap is. So many club golfers suffer from delusions of grandeur in these circumstances, attempting shots that would make Arnold Palmer pale under his tan. Arnold Palmer has always been a fantastic recovery player, immensely strong and with a real ability to work out the most difficult shots and execute them to perfection. At the same time he has a very cool head and will not be drawn into attempting the impossible.

Faced with the situation illustrated here, you must weigh your likely chances of success with the penalties involved if you fail. In going for the green you must get the ball quickly into the air to clear the branches of the tree in front of you and hit the ball far enough on this high trajectory to clear the lake between you and the hole. A steep bank at the front of the green will throw a short shot back towards the water and if you should get the ball flying well, as you are likely to do from short rough you could well finish in the deep bunker

at the back of the green. If the ball is lying well you may be tempted to try the bold shot. But what about the wind blowing fairly strongly in your face? Can you use it as a safety factor which will allow you to hit the ball hard with little fear of overshooting the green, or is it likely to hold up your high-flying shot and drop it short of the target? Now you should

consider what will happen if you fail to execute the shot to perfection. If the ball clips the branches in front of you the ball may finish up short of the lake, in which case you are still faced with a difficult shot, or in the lake, meaning the difficult shot and a one-shot penalty. If you catch the bank at the front of the green you have a chance of staying out of the water, but an awkward pitch shot up the bank to a close pin position. By overshooting into the trap at the back of the green you will then be faced with a tricky sand shot with the lake looming close behind the pin.

In a medal round, you may well decide that the risks make this an impractical shot and you will chip out sideways to the fairway and accept the fact that you may drop one shot, but you certainly will not lose two or three, which would be a real possibility if you took the bold approach.

On the other hand, in match play, where your opponent is on the green in two shots and your second shot has landed you in the position we show here, then you will almost certainly decide that the only answer is to attack the hole. If playing safe is not going to achieve anything you should settle yourself correctly, maintain your swing rhythm and go for the kill.

OVER AND UNDER

The ability to hit high and low shots can be extremely useful in a variety of situations on the golf course, not only when you are faced with shots over and under trees as illustrated here.

There are times when you want an approach shot to the green to clear a sand trap and stop quickly. Out of semi-rough you will not be able to generate the amount of backspin necessary to achieve this, but a shot which climbs quickly with a high, lobbing trajectory, can land very softly and give the same result. Low shots, on the other hand, can be real shot-savers when looking for accuracy against or across a strong wind.

Before we go into the specific techniques for each shot we should look at the general implications of what we are trying to achieve. To get the ball high we need more loft on the clubface and to hit the ball low we require less loft. In the early part of the book we discovered that a change in ball position in relation to the feet also had an effect on the position of the hands in relation to the clubhead and to the amount of clubface loft.

In playing shots from sand, we placed the ball well forward in the stance, thus bringing the hands level with the clubhead rather than in front of it, and by opening the clubface we further

high

124

increased the loft. These are the techniques we use for hitting high and low shots.

To get the ball up quickly it should be placed well forward in the stance, perhaps just inside the left heel. This means that the hands are level with the clubhead rather than ahead as they would be for a normal wedge shot. This will increase the loft of the clubface and if you want the ball to get up exceptionally fast you can help it still further by opening the clubface slightly.

The grip on the club should be light to encourage more use of the hands in picking the clubhead up quickly on the backswing and in delivering it back to the ball sharply with plenty of hand action. The overall impression is that this is very much a hand swing. To keep the ball low we must follow the opposite procedure, moving the ball back in the stance until it is just past the midway point between the feet. This effectively puts the hands well ahead of the clubhead and reduces the amount of loft on the clubface. The key to these shots is to reproduce this position at impact. There is a restricted amount of hand action in this type of shot and the feeling should be one of a firm-wristed swing with the arms doing most of the work. The weight must be well on to the left side before impact.

The high shot will tend to fade the ball off to the right and the low shot will draw the ball to the left.

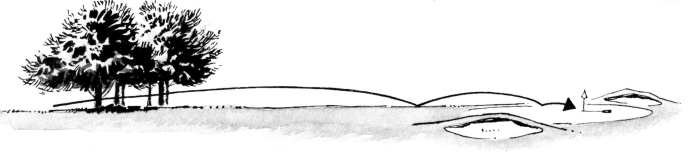

The worst aspect of playing shots from the rough is that you do not have as much control over the ball as you do when playing from the fairway. The intrusion of grass between the clubhead and the ball means an imprecise contact which will always mean less backspin and less control. Often you will get what is known as a 'flier.' This is when the ball seems to leap off the clubface and continues to roll a long way once it has pitched.

Common sense must play a large part in the way you play recovery shots from the rough. Each shot should be judged on its merits, but do not try the impossible when the ball is deeply embedded in six inches of grass. In these circumstances a wedge shot back to the fairway is the best you can hope for. Obviously you need a lofted club to get the ball up out of the thicker rough and the basic tactic with this type of shot is to keep the clubface out of the grass as much as possible. This means that the backswing and downswing should be steep.

PLAYING OUT OF THE ROUGH

The ball should be positioned back in the middle of the stance to encourage a quick pick up in the backswing and a downward blow into the ball. It would be impossible to sweep the clubhead away from the ball on a low arc because it would get tangled up in the grass and this is the very last thing you want, either in the backswing or downswing. Pick the club up steeply in the backswing with an early break of the wrists, but beware of collapsing the left arm. Keep the weight largely on the left side throughout the shot and bring the clubhead back steeply into the ball, trying to keep the clubhead out of the grass until you have made contact with the ball. You will need a firm left hand grip for these shots.

It seems likely that contact with the grass will force the face of the club open at impact, but the reverse is true. In longer rough the grass clings around the heel and the hosel of the club and forces the clubface closed. Be prepared for this and, if necessary, aim off to the right of your target.

In really deep rough aim at the back of the ball with a downward, chopping action and don't worry about a follow through. Just try to make as sharp a contact with the ball as possible—and, of course, be aiming at the nearest point of safety.

This is an area of the game which most golfers never practice and that may account for some of the poor recovery play you see everywhere. It is well worth a few minutes of your time to try various shots from medium and deep rough so that you at least have an idea of how the ball will react under certain circumstances. What you must prove to yourself as soon as possible is that you will get no results at all if you try to scoop the ball out of the rough. You must hit down.

through impact.

The real tricky ones are standing above or below the ball. With the ball below the feet you must avoid the normal reaction of bending over from the waist. You must retain your normal address posture and the only way you can do this and get the clubhead behind the ball is to flex the knees more than usual. A slightly open stance will help you to hit through impact, where a normal square stance tends to get the left side of the body in the way of the arms and club. The ball will tend to fade so you should aim off left. With the ball on a higher level than the feet you will have to choke down on the grip of the club in order to adopt as normal a posture as possible. Correct weight distribution and balance are very important and these shots will have a tendency to hook so you should make compensation by aiming slightly right of your target.

Getting out of trouble

Deliberately hooking or fading the ball is something many handicap players will feel is a little out of their league, but there is a simple technique which I recommend you should try on the practice tee. This can be invaluable in shaping shots around bushes and trees. To fade the ball all you need do is open the stance, aiming feet and shoulders to the left, and then concentrate solely on increasing the grip pressure in the first two fingers of each hand. This has the effect of cutting down slightly on the hand action. By keeping the key thought simple and working from the right set-up you will be surprised how much more easy these shots are than you imagined. To reverse the shape of the ball, in other words to hook it, you adopt exactly the reverse procedure. Close the stance by aiming the feet and shoulders to the right of your target and concentrate the grip pressure at the back of the hands, in the last two or three fingers.

That covers the normal day-to-day problem shots which plague everyone who takes up this wonderful but often frustrating game. However, there are a few other shot-savers that I would like to pass on, even though you may come across them only occasionally in your golf. On the basis that it is sensible to be prepared for every eventuality it is certainly worth thinking about some of the worst situations that can confront you.

Water presents one of the most penal hazards in golf, although there are times when the ball is not lost in the depths, but sitting tantalisingly partly submerged or just under the surface around the edges of a lake or stream. You must consider carefully whether to accept a penalty shot and drop the ball clear of the water or whether it is worth getting slightly wet to save a match. If you do decide to play the ball as it lies, put on your waterproof clothing. Not only will this prevent a most uncomfortable end to the round, it will also improve your confidence and help you to hit firmly into the ball. You need to follow basically the same principles from water as you would with a recovery shot from sand. Where the ball is partly above the surface of the water you have no real problem in delivering the clubhead

DEFEATING THE OBSTACLES

You may consider that deliberately hooking or slicing shots around obstructions is pretty advanced technique. In fact, if you have followed the logical progression of instruction throughout the book you will be able to achieve these shots quite easily.

As with every shot in golf, we must set ourselves at address in the position we wish to repeat at impact. Going back once again to our comparison with rifle shooting, you must aim the weapon before you pull the trigger. You would not, for instance, deliberately aim ten yards to the right of the target and then try to swing the rifle into position as you

were taking up the trigger pressure. Exactly the same thing is true in golf. You should not set up the body in one position and then try to make changes once you have started to swing the club.

For all shots, and more particularly the difficult ones, it is essential to be in the correct position before you start and to have one key thought in mind which will help you to complete the shot correctly. We can do this with the 'professional'

shots like deliberate hooks and fades.

Confronted with a green completely hidden by the trees and the distance between you and the trees too great to contemplate flying the ball straight over the top, you have the choice of trying to bend the ball round this obstacle from either side. What should influence your decision?

First, you will have a natural feel for which shot comes more easily to you and second, you should look at the likely landing point of the ball should you fail to bend it all the way around to the green. Always take the route which gives the biggest safety margin. Take the trouble to practice these shots – don't wait until you are confronted with a tricky situation on the course before you try something new. In this way you will have some confidence in your ability to move the ball either way, for there are many situations which will not offer you a choice.

To fade the ball from the left, open up the stance at address, with the line through the feet, hips and shoulders pointing to the left. We know from our earlier analysis that this is a set-up which will encourage a slice. Ensure that your swing rhythm is normal, don't be tempted into rushing things because you are doing something slightly different. And your key thought here should be to concentrate a firm grip in the first two fingers of each hand. This will effectively cut down on your hand action and hit the ball with a slightly open clubface. The ball will not fly as far as normal so make sure you have enough club.

To hook the ball round from the right we adopt the reverse procedure, closing up the stance, pointing to the right of the target line, and the grip pressure should be concentrated in the last two fingers of each hand. This will give you lively hand action and get the clubface through the ball in a slightly closed position. In this instance the ball will run further than usual, so make the necessary allowances.

Try these shots on your next practice session. You may only need to make use of them once in every ten rounds, but if they save a shot every time it will be worth it.

Just as difficult as the uphill and downward lies are those situations where the ball is either above or below your feet. Once again the key to success lies in the ability to adopt the correct position at address. Whenever you are faced with a situation where you and the ball are not on level ground there must be adjustments made in the address positon so that your ability to swing the club freely through the ball is as close to that for a normal level-ground shot as possible.

It is a strange thing, but even golfers of reasonable playing ability seem reluctant to work out the problems posed by shots from sloping ground. There is usually a fairly simple remedy if common sense and logic are applied.

For instance, where the ball is well below the feet, a normal set-up will produce a swing which will, at best, make contact with the top half of the

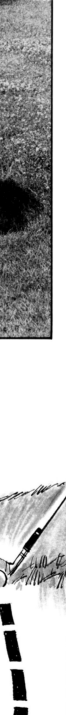

ball. The only factor which differentiates this shot from a regular iron shot from level ground is the distance between the player and the ball. Quite obviously if the ball is below the level of the feet we must do something at address to rectify this imbalance. There are only two possibilities – and unfortunately the majority of club golfers choose the wrong one. How often

have you seen players in this situation with their legs almost straight and a tremendous bend at the waist in order to get the clubhead behind the ball?

The real answer lies in taking a perfectly normal position and then flexing the knees just as much as is necessary for the clubhead to rest comfortably behind the ball. Almost invariably these shots will fade off to the right during

their flight so you should line up at the left edge of your target to compensate.

In the reverse situation, with the ball above the level of the feet, there is only one way you can swing normally and not catch the ground behind the ball. You must shorten the distance between your left shoulder and the ball. The way to do this is to choke down on the grip of the

club, just as we learned to do when digging our feet well into the sand for trap shots. Grip down on the club and you can swing in the normal way. This shot will tend to hook, so aim off right and allow for it.

It is very important, when playing both these shots, to take a couple of practice swings while standing close to the ball. You practice swing must be on the same slope as the shot you are about to hit. In this way you can judge correctly the amount of knee flex required or just how far down the grip you must hold the club. Your practice swings should have the head of the club clipping the turf so that you can then step forward to the real shot with confidence.

behind the ball, but when it is completely submerged you have a further problem—light refraction. Because light rays are bent as they pass through water the ball will always appear to be closer to the surface than it is. Therefore you must swing the clubhead to hit a point slightly lower than the balls appears.

Left-handed skills

Another useful weapon to have up your sleeve is the ability to get the ball out of trouble spots left-handed. Everyone has faced the situation where the ball is tight up against a tree or under the overhanging branches of a bush and it is absolutely impossible to play the shot right-handed. Rather than declaring the ball un-playable and collecting a penalty stroke, you will often be able to move the ball a reasonable distance by playing a left-handed shot. The best solution is to reverse a fairly straight-faced club so that the toe of the blade rests on the ground behind the ball. Before getting into position to play the shot you will need two or three practice swings to overcome the strangeness of swinging the wrong way round. The one thing you must not do is rush the shot. You should keep the backswing short—not more than half a swing—but retain your natural rhythm. A gentle, evenly paced swing will achieve better results than a quick stab which is the more natural reaction. The shot can be played with your normal grip or by reversing the position of the hands and placing the left hand below the right, whichever feels most comfortable and gives you the most control. As with all trouble shots it is worth a few minutes at the end of a practice session to try this left-handed escape route.

Wet grass and rough

Although short rough does not, at first sight, appear to present much of a hazard, it can, in fact, ruin many shots to the green because of the unpredictable way in which the ball may behave. Very often from wet grass you will get a 'flyer' as it is known – a ball which shoots off the clubface and runs through the green. This is caused by the wet grass getting between the ball and the face of the club and reducing the amount of backspin on the ball. This means it will often fly further than normal and lacks any form of control when it pitches. At other times a delicate pitch or chip shot can be upset because a golfer is not certain how much the grass will affect the clubhead at impact. That is why I would advise every golfer to practise shots from the rough with a number of clubs so that, at least, he had some idea of the likely outcome before encountering the situation on the golf course in the middle of a competitive round.

It is particularly important with short shots and you should not hesitate to practice from light rough at a range of about 20 yards. Set out a target with a couple of clubs and try a whole range of shots to see which gives the best results. Experiment from the sand-wedge down to the seven and six-irons. The important point is to know, in advance, the type of reaction you will get on the course.

DOWNHILL AND UPHILL

Because they don't pose the same problems as manufacturing shots from under trees, over lakes or round bushes, there is a tendency to treat uphill and downhill shots with a lack of concentration and thought. In reality, they can be just as difficult as the more obvious trouble shots and they certainly need to be played with the correct technique.

In both cases the key to success lies in your ability to adopt the correct set-up position. There is a natural tendency to lean into the slope to maintain balance, for both uphill and downhill shots. What you must attempt to achieve

is a body position which is as near as possible at right angles to the slope of the ground. In other words we are trying to duplicate conditions for a normal shot from level ground.

The trouble is that if you adopt a normal address position at right angles to the slope and with the weight evenly balanced between the feet, you will be totally off balance by the time you reach the top of your backswing. Somehow we have to make compensations to transfer part of the body

weight into the slope while retaining the ideal body position. In this way we shall be able to swing through the ball in an unhindered fashion and still retain the balance which is essential for every golf shot.

The way we can do this is to use the legs and hips as the balancing factors, leaving the upper body in its correct perpendicular position.

When playing up a slope, the left leg should flex more than the right and the weight should be pushed forward more onto the left hip. From this balanced position you will find that you can now try to set you body at right angles to the slope. This will mean that you can sweep the head of the club away down the slope in the backswing and will have a completely free through swing, past impact. The clubhead should now be able to swing correctly through impact and again follow the contour of the slope past the ball. If the entire body is allowed to lean into the slope the clubhead will not be able to swing through the ball, but will stab quickly into the ground just past impact.

When the slope is dropping away from you, the right leg should be flexed more than the left and the weight held back slightly towards the right side. It is more difficult here to get the body at right angles to the slope and you will almost invariably find that you do, in fact, lean back slightly to the right. This will cause no great harm as long as it is not overdone for this will lead to hitting the ball thin. As with the uphill shots the clubhead should move back from the ball along the slope and after impact you should have the distinct impression of the club-head following the ball down the slope. In both shots you may find it helpful to widen the stance slightly to assist proper balance.

Strategy on and off the course

Guard against your weaknesses and exploit your strengths. At the end of the day you need to return a capable score. Try to avoid desperate situations which demand over extended strokes.

If you consider that every shot you play in golf is designed to make the next shot as easy as possible, you have virtually mastered the art of intelligent strategy and shot planning. Think before you play. Common sense can save you shots in every round.

Your golf course strategy should start the moment you shut the office door behind you. I know that like all amateurs you just don't have the time to get to the course an hour before you play so that you can hit a bagful of balls in a warm-up session. If you cannot go through the ideal routine that the tournament professionals use, then you must do everything else possible to get into the right mental and physical shape on the first tee. As you drive to the course you can start to relax your shoulder and arm muscles, begin to ease the tension from your neck that inevitably builds up during business. Now is the time to start your mental preparation as well. Try to imagine yourself on the first tee getting ready to start your round. The chances are that you will be playing on your home course and that you will be able to visualise vividly the hole as it stretches away from you. Are you going to play it with the driver today? How confident do you feel about hitting the fairway? Is it necessary to hit driver, or can you open up with the three-wood and still get home safely?

These are the thoughts which should be occupying your mind on your way to the club. Picture yourself playing the opening holes and set yourself a realistic target score for the first three holes. If the first is a par-four which always gives you trouble then why don't you set it in your mind as a par-five and be content to make five. So often you can harm your mental attitude right at the start of a round and this will affect your performance for the entire 18 holes. Just remember that every handicap player is expected to drop shots—that is why he has a handicap. If you set yourself a realistic target, expecting to drop some shots, particularly over the opening holes, then you will not feel disappointed and your mental attitude will remain positive.

The jinx hole
As amateurs who play most of their golf over the same course you have a real opportunity to study the dangers and pitfalls and plan your golf correctly. How often have you heard a player admit that he can never play a particular hole well? You may have a jinx hole of your own. But have you ever stopped to think why. Do you still play it the same way every time or have you tried a different plan of attack. The chances are that you try the same thing round after round, just like beating your head against a wall. Always remember that you can almost certainly play the majority of par-five holes by hitting three five-irons. Golf is a thinking game, not just one of brute power. There are many ways to play every golf hole ever designed and you should always be looking to use the parts of your game which are the strongest and to eliminate those where you are not so proficient.

Go back over your last few rounds in your mind and jot down the shots and the holes which cost you strokes. Do you struggle for distance and accuracy off the tee but make up your score with a slick short game and good putting? Or are you one of those players who suffers the frustration of hitting good shots to the green and failing to make any kind of putt? You may well never have stopped to analyse the strengths and weaknesses of your own game.

What I want you to realise is that if a certain drive always catches you out, if you always finish in deep rough and wind up with a six or worse, then there is no rule in the book which says you can't hit a four-iron off the tee and make your attack on the hole from a different angle. Never be frightened to change the pattern of your play in this way. You see the pros do it all the time in tournaments.

The last hole of the US Open Championship at Inverness, in 1979, a short par-four with a narrow dog-legged fairway and heavily bunkered sloping green, had the professionals using anything from a driver to a two-iron off the tee. The objective in every case was to get the ball into a position from which the best score could be made. I often feel that club golfers lose sight of this objective, reaching automatically for the driver at any hole which is not a par-three.

What you have to avoid at all costs is a negative attitude. Work out a plan of campaign for each hole and each shot and tackle it in a positive and possibly an attacking manner. The game is much more fun this way.

Reaching the end

So this is the day when you and I play our final round together. As usual you have arrived at the first tee without time for a pre-round warm-up—it was another hard morning at the office. We have to do something to get you quickly into the right mental and physical shape. The best way I know for you to loosen up your tight muscles is to go through a few simple exercises with one or two golf clubs. As it is the golfing muscles we want to warm up let's do some golfing-type exercises. I like to hold two clubs by the neck in the left hand and the grips in the right and swing them round my body in order to get the kinks out of my back. Putting a club behind your back, with both elbows hooked round it, the one you so often see Jack Nicklaus going through on the first tee, is also an excellent warm-up. You can go through your normal backswing and through swing turn with the club in this position, pointing the end of the shaft at the ball on the backswing and the other end of the club at the ball on the through swing.

The final loosener before we get down to the real thing is to take a dozen or so slow, easy swings with two clubs. This not only works on the muscles but also on the mind. The rhythm has to be slow and easy with two clubs, there is no way you can rush it. This is one of the best ways of setting yourself into the swing tempo you will want to use on the course.

As for the mental side, we have already discussed the possibility of setting your own personal par score for the opening holes. Don't expect miracles—they don't happen too often in golf. Set realistic but demanding targets for the first three holes and get yourself into a positive frame of mind. Now it is time to study the first hole in detail, and the real answer is to work back from the pin position. If the pin is tucked behind a bunker on the left side of the green you will ideally want to play into the green from the right side of the fairway. This means that the best starting point for your tee shot is as far left as you can go between the tee markers, do get into this position if it is possible.

One of the main differences between the scene at an average golf club at the weekend and the same club during the week of a major professional tournament will be the amount of activity on the practice tee. On a normal weekend it is almost unused. During a pro event every contestant will use the practice area before each round, and very often afterwards as well.

I accept the fact that we are playing for a living and would be very stupid indeed not to arrive on the first tee in the best possible shape. On the other hand you only play for fun – but how much more fun could you have by playing to something like you best ability from the first tee rather than wasting the first four or five holes in an on-course warm-up.

It can be difficult to make enough time, or to raise enough enthusiasm to spend an hour on the practice tee before each match. This is approximately the amount of time each pro takes to run through the key clubs in the bag and leave ten minutes for putting and chipping practice. I am not suggesting that one hour is necessary at club level, but I would urge any of you who are really keen to improve your scoring to devote 10 to 15 minutes

to a warm-up session before you play. Start with a few loosening up swings, then hit a few wedge and short-iron shots. If possible, work your way up through the

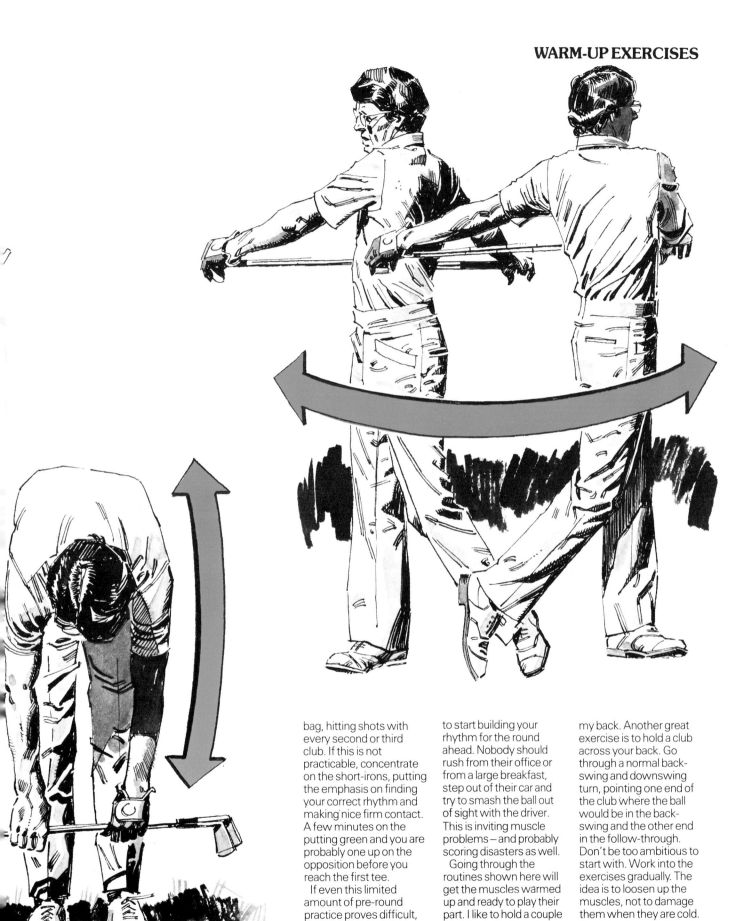

bag, hitting shots with every second or third club. If this is not practicable, concentrate on the short-irons, putting the emphasis on finding your correct rhythm and making nice firm contact. A few minutes on the putting green and you are probably one up on the opposition before you reach the first tee.

If even this limited amount of pre-round practice proves difficult, then please spend five minutes on the few simples exercises shown here. The purpose is two-fold. First to loosen the muscles and second to start building your rhythm for the round ahead. Nobody should rush from their office or from a large breakfast, step out of their car and try to smash the ball out of sight with the driver. This is inviting muscle problems – and probably scoring disasters as well.

Going through the routines shown here will get the muscles warmed up and ready to play their part. I like to hold a couple of clubs, with the grips in one hand and the heads in the other and then swing them round slowly at full arm stretch. This one really gets the kinks out of my back. Another great exercise is to hold a club across your back. Go through a normal back-swing and downswing turn, pointing one end of the club where the ball would be in the back-swing and the other end in the follow-through. Don't be too ambitious to start with. Work into the exercises gradually. The idea is to loosen up the muscles, not to damage them when they are cold. Start slowly and without turning too far and gradually increase the turn as you feel the resistance in the muscles begin to relax.

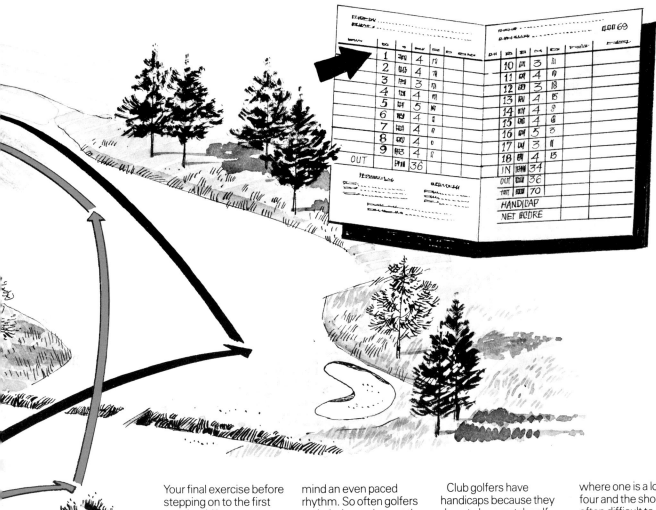

Your final exercise before stepping on to the first tee should be to go through the full swing with two clubs. Having loosened the muscles with our earlier routines we should now be putting this into golfing perspective. Our final exercise is a combination of preparing the muscles and the mind.

It is impossible to swing two clubs quickly. You must place them very deliberately at the top of the backswing and allow the additional weight to help swing down and through to a high finish. Start these swings with your feet together and everything will start to fall into place very quickly. After half a dozen swings you can widen the stance and really feel the rhythm of the swing.

Not only does this routine give the final boost to the muscles, taking them through the full swing cycle, but it helps establish in your mind an even paced rhythm. So often golfers rush their tee shots at the first hole, purely because they have done nothing to prepare their muscles or their rhythm.

Just as important as your physical preparation is a positive mental attitude which will help you to play to the best of your ability. This does not mean an attack-at-all-costs policy. It means a sensible assessment of your own strengths and weaknesses in relation to the course and your state of play. I often see mid and high-handicap players in a dejected state after three or four holes because they started cold and suddenly found they had dropped four or five shots to par. A few minutes devoted to a pre-round warm-up and a more realistic approach to their own scoring ability could have turned this situation into the start of a very enjoyable round of golf.

Club golfers have handicaps because they do not play scratch golf. They must expect to drop shots – and where more likely than in the opening holes if they have made no attempt to prepare properly. Even if you give yourself enough time for the few simple exercises I have outlined in this chapter you will still not be ready to attack the course from the opening hole. You must learn to play within your ability, particularly at the start of a round.

Allocate your own par figures to groups of three holes at a time. If you are a 14 handicap player, you can expect to drop shots at all but four holes on the course. If you are five over after four holes, why be depressed? If the opening holes at your course are difficult to negotiate you can safely allow your own personal par figures to reflect this. Say the first three holes are four, four, three,

where one is a long par four and the short hole is often difficult to reach. If you set your own target as six, five, four and you stand on the fourth tee less than four over par you will continue the round with a much better mental attitude. In your own mind you will be winning – and your chances of improving on your handicap will be much better.

In the first hole shown here the opening shot of the day would have to be a good one to clear the stream. If it were the tenth hole you would probably not hesitate to take out the driver. But I would suggest you will get off to a more satisfactory start if you hit the tee shot with a three or four-wood, lay up short of the green in two and then pitch or chip on. Without straining any muscles or your early-hole ability you could still make four, almost certainly a five.

You have all seen the cartoon showing a sign writer painting a notice which says 'think ahead' — only he has not allowed sufficient room to complete the second word. A lot of golf is played that way at club level. It is amazing how many players reach unthinkingly for the driver at any hole that is not a par-three, and the only thought in their mind is to get the ball somewhere in the fairway.

Not even the tournament pros hit the ball exactly where they want it to go with every shot, but at least they have picked a definite aiming point. If they do hit it correctly then they finish in the prime position. It is a tragic waste for a handicap golfer to hit his best shot with the driver, only to find that he does not have a clear shot to the green because his planning was poor or non-existent. A little thought can save you a handful of shots in each round.

Each shot in golf should be played with the intention of making the next shot as easy as possible. As with the management of little shots around the green we must logically work back from the position of the hole. At the par-five hole shown here the pin is tucked behind a sand trap on the left side of the green. This means that the safe route for the third shot is to come in from the right side of the fairway. To place the ball there, the drive should be hit down the left side of the fairway. The solid lines show the sensible, safe way to play this hole and the black lines show the way it will be tackled by the golfer who does no planning at all. By going down the centre of the fairway in a direct line to the green you will be faced with an approach shot which must be played uphill over a large bunker. This is a difficult shot to judge and one which will make it very difficult to get the ball close to the hole.

Our thinking golfer will have a relatively easy shot with plenty of green on which to pitch the ball. Even if he does not hit a good approach shot he will still be on the green with two putts for a par, where the player who took the more direct route will have been tempting fate all the way from tee to green, playing too close to the trees from the tee and with his second shot. If he negotiates these safely he still has a very real chance of dropping his third shot into the sand trap and he is unlikely to make better than a six from that position.

Every time you stand on a tee you must look ahead, where possible, to the green and work out your strategy in reverse order.

This is the type of short par-four hole you encounter on almost every golf course, offering a choice between staying on the safe and narrow fairway or getting much closer to the green by cutting across the trees on the corner of the dogleg.

What advantages can you gain by cutting the corner with a big tee shot? You will obviously have a much shorter shot to the green and therefore a better chance of getting the ball closer to the hole. Yet once again the position of the hole on the green will play a vital part in your shot planning. With the pin hidden close behind the trap on the left of the green a short cut across the corner will still leave you with a difficult second shot. Is it worth the risk? The answer, almost certainly, is no.

Yet if the pin was in the right half of the green and you were hitting the ball well you might well be justified in going for the big drive and setting up the chance of a birdie. Yet you must always be aware of the dangers of such a shot before you make your decision. If the tee shot fails and you finish under the trees on the corner of the dogleg you must face the fact that you will almost certainly not be able to make the green with your second shot.

If you have any doubts in your mind you should not attempt the more difficult shot. You need to be hitting the ball well and to have absolute confidence in your ability before you take short-cuts of this nature. Any lingering doubts in your mind will almost certainly upset your rhythm.

Playing the hole in the straightforward manner will call for an accurate tee shot which must not be too long. This will probably mean a four or five-wood off the tee, or even an iron shot. The priority is to hit the area of fairway which will give you a clear sight of the green. Any club which will allow you to achieve this is the right

club for the job. There is no disgrace in playing for position with an iron. This is what the game is all about. You make a good score by hitting shots into the best positions – and this can be achieved with

a variety of clubs.

Two useful points arise from playing the hole in this way. All the trouble is on the left side from the tee, so you should tee the ball as far left as you can go between the tee

markers. This means that you are aiming the ball away from trouble. This is a golden rule which you should always follow. The second point is the club selection for the second shot. There is a universal

tendency to underclub for shots to the green. In this example the green is very large and it is far better to be putting from the back of the green than chipping from short of the front edge.

This is the type of shot planning which can make such a big difference to a score at the end of the day, yet so few handicap golfers give it a thought. Plan every hole in this way, taking into account the wind conditions, position of bunkers and trees and then concentrate hard on each shot in an effort to make them fit your plan. One very important factor is the position on the tee from which you hit your drive. If there is any sort of trouble on the hole you should tee up on the same side as the trees or the out-of-bounds and hit away from it. This gives you a much greater margin of safety and is something you will almost always see the tournament pros doing. The few exceptions will be when a player wants to hit a particular shape of shot for some reason.

The very long holes
Par-five holes can be a real hang-up for many club players. They would do well to remember that not too many pros hit the par-five greens in two shots. It is no disgrace to take three or even four shots at these holes, so plan sensibly, not necessarily trying to thrash the ball out of sight with the biggest clubs in your bag. If you are not struggling to hit a five-iron to the green, but have got yourself in a comfortable position somewhere close to the putting surface you will then have a chance to manage the next shot more precisely. This can mean ensuring that the ball finishes below rather than above the hole, thus lessening the chances of wasting putts.

Guarding against your weaknesses and exploiting your strengths is what the game is all about. If, for instance, you are not yet an accomplished bunker player, but you have some very good control with chip shots, you might be well advised to hit approach shots well wide of any bunkers, avoiding your weaknesses and exploiting your strength to make the best score. Because that's what it is all about at the end of the day. Unless you are in a desperate match-play situation which demands boldness you will find better results game after game by hitting for the safest part of the green rather than attacking the pin.

In the Open Championship at Royal Lytham St Annes in 1979 most of the world's top professional players were hitting for the fat part of the greens and not taking too many chances. Playing in pro-am events I often get the chance to find out the way that amateur golfers think about the game. A typical situation will be that a man has a club in his hand which I know very well will not get him to the green—and all the trouble is at the front of the green. When I ask why he is hitting that club I often get the answer that it is a club he hits well and he is unsure about the bigger clubs. Yet he is almost certainly hitting himself into trouble with his favourite club. Doesn't make too much sense does it?

There are three things during the course of a round of golf which let down most players—and I see them repeated week after week in pro-am events and back at my home club.

Players are mainly guilty of poor planning, imagining they can achieve shots which are clearly beyond them, or no planning at all; very many of them aim off to the right without realising

PAR THREE FINESSE

The decision you face on the tee at every short hole is whether to play for the hole or for the safe part of the green. On the longer par-threes you may want to look at the safe areas just short of the green if you are not confident of reaching the putting surface with your tee shot.

Distance and accuracy are vital on these holes and this is where your practice ground routine of checking the length you hit with each club is really going to pay dividends. If you are unsure of which club to hit you will almost certainly finish up with a poor shot. If the underlying feeling at the back of your mind is that you have too much club in your hands then you will make sloppy, decelerating contact with the ball and any type of shot can result – usually a weak hit which will fall short of the target. If, on the other hand, you have a suspicion that you have underclubbed yourself you will rush into the ball, destroying your swing rhythm in an attempt to squeeze a few extra yards from the club.

Being confident that you have the right club in your hands is more than half the battle on these holes. You will be able to concentrate all your attention on making a full rhythmic swing. This will aid your accuracy as there will be no attempts to ease or force the shot.

At the short hole illustrated here, the lake protects the right half of the green which also narrows down considerably on the right side, giving rise to some very difficult pin placements on a narrow neck of green beyond the water. In almost every circumstance you should take the safe route across dry land to the fat part of the green. Only in matchplay, with your opponent close to the hole and in a commanding position, should you attempt the direct line at the pin. However poor your shot on the left-hand route you will still have a chance to make three. The slightest error when aiming at the pin will drop you in the water or put the ball off the back of the green.

The strength and direction of the wind can make a very real difference to the way you play the short holes. It is not always easy to judge how strong the wind is and often you will be playing from a sheltered tee to an exposed green. As shown in the example here, the ball may only catch the wind when it rises above tree height. Watch for all the tell-tale signs. Always look at the flag to see how much it is moving. Study the tops of the trees to see how much effect the wind is having at that height — and remember that as your ball nears the target and loses its forward momentum the wind will have its greatest influence. Be aware of all these factors and use them in your assessment of the shot to be played.

it; and almost everyone underclubs. Get those three things sorted out and you could be scoring two or three shots better very quickly.

I nearly discovered to my cost in the final round of the 1979 US Open the folly of not thinking in a positive fashion. With a five-shot lead I suddenly realised that I was thinking only of not letting it slip away—and it began to do just that. It took a real mental nudge to get myself back into the frame of mind where I put full positive concentration into each shot in turn and each hole as it came.

Stick to your positive thoughts and plan each shot carefully and you are well on the way to overcoming the experience which every golfer goes through at some time in his golfing life— scoring badly at the final crucial holes after playing extremely well up to that point.

Pressure in golf

There are all sorts of pressures in golf, from the ones I have endured in winning Open Championships to those which every player has faced when he needs a four or five at the last hole for the best score of his life. The cause of the pressure may be very different, yet the experience is no less real or crucial for you than for me. Clear your mind of any irrelevant thoughts. Get your cone of concentration closing in on the ball and the target and picture clearly the shot you intend to play. Take a couple of practice swings while concentrating solely on the rhythm of your swing. If your rhythm deserts you now you will not hit the shot you need. If necessary take a couple of swings with your feet together to ensure that you are thinking positively along the right lines. Then take a deep, relaxing breath and hit it.

Because golf is played in a cold-blooded fashion, with each shot being closely studied on its own merits, unlike the fast reaction sports where you only have minimal time to get into position and make your play, it does add considerably to the mental pressures. I believe very strongly that rhythm and balance are the links between the physical and mental sides of golf and these are the first factors to suffer when we cannot handle the pressure. The more we can do to retain our swing rhythm at times of stress the better we shall play the important shots.

Keep your rhythm

In my experience the best way to keep a cool head and a steady rhythm is to follow exactly a regular pattern which you have built up in your practice and play. Take a practice swing, line up the shot, adjust your stance and grip in the same way you always do and mentally you are becoming tuned to a normal shot—you are doing everything possible to eliminate the rhythm-destroying tension which a critical shot can so easily bring about. If Billy Casper is disturbed as he is about to play a shot he will step away from the ball and put the club back in the bag, even to the extent of replacing the head cover. He clears his mind completely, takes another look at the target, takes the club from the bag and goes through his normal build-up routine again. In this way he prepares himself mentally for a difficult situation.

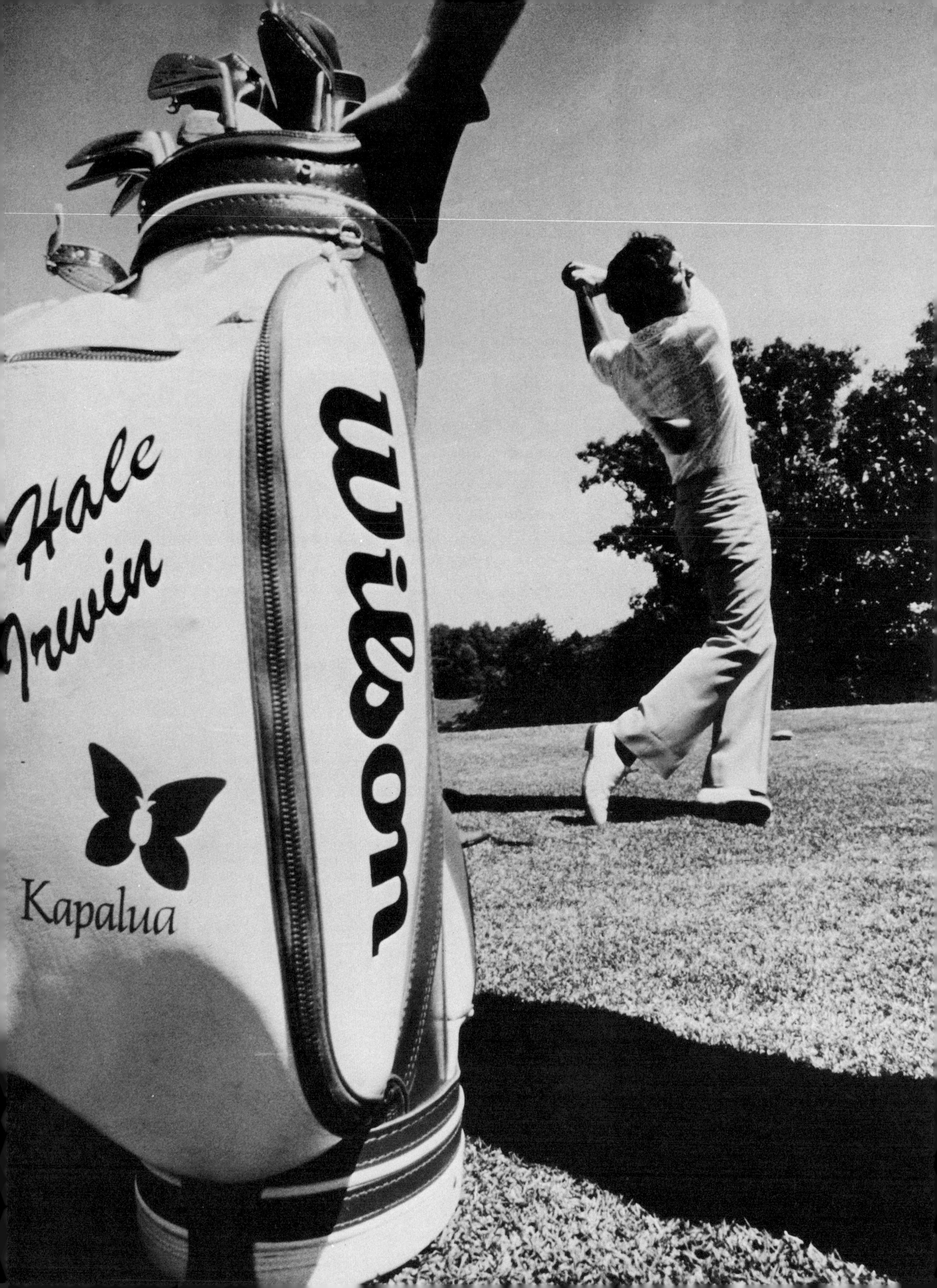
Hale Irwin
Kapalua
Wilson

Equipment: choose carefully

Do not burden yourself with inferior or ill-fitting equipment. Do not be afraid to experiment to find the right type of gear. The correct mental attitude can be created by the right appearance.

The range of golf equipment available today is so extensive that you need to study the market very carefully before buying. Looking after your clubs and other equipment can also help make it last longer and help you play better.

Considering what you expect from your golf equipment there seems to be a general lack of attention to its selection and care. I am not suggesting that you can buy a perfect golf game in the pro shop, but you can buy good quality equipment to suit your own particular needs and this will help you to produce the best golf of which you are capable. Golf can be quite difficult enough without the additional handicap of inferior or ill-fitting equipment. You should always give yourself the maximum chance of playing your best. Good equipment is an important factor in this. As with the basic fundamentals of the golf swing, there are certain parameters in the choice of equipment within which you should work. These relate to the length, lie, flex and weight of the clubs which suit you. And when all these factors have been considered the clubs must appear good looking to you. They must be pleasing to look at so that you feel confident at address. Oddly enough the regular length of golf shaft is ideal for a vast number of people of varying builds. It is, on average, very seldom necessary for people to have lengthened or shortened clubs. The reason for this is quite simple when you look at the way people are made. The taller person will normally have fairly long arms and as you come down in size, so the shorter person has shorter arms. We are all made in approximately the same proportions and the distance at which our hands hang from the ground is astonishingly constant throughout an enormous difference of overall heights. However, should you find it necessary to bend over from the waist or to flex the knees more than the acceptable amount because the grips of your clubs are just not close enough to you, then you will undoubtedly benefit from extra length shafts. If, on the other hand, you are forced to choke down on every grip because your clubs are uncomfortably long, then you, too, are not getting the best from your equipment.

Special clubs

What you need is a special order of clubs made specifically to your length. This is not normally more expensive than ordering a standard set—though it might take a little longer to get delivery. What you should be careful of is having clubs shortened or plugs inserted in the end of the shaft as both these remedies will effect the original balance, overall weight and swing weight of the clubs. In addition to the length of the shaft there is another aspect which is concerned purely with technical specification as opposed to feel. This is the lie of the club, the angle at which the clubhead is set on the shaft. The regular lie will suit the vast majority of golfers, but there will be those who will benefit from an adjustment. If you find the toe of the club is lifting off the ground as you address the ball you could well be one of those who need a slightly flatter lie than that used on most production clubs. Very occasionally a tall player with a very upright swing will need a more upright lie than normal. These specific areas should be discussed with your golf pro, who will be only too happy to tell you whether you are getting the best from the regular range of clubs. The other two areas where you might wish to try something different are in the flex of the shaft and the swing-weight of the clubs. These are factors which affect the feel of the clubs in your hands. In fact the shaft is the most important part of any golf club. If the shaft is of good quality you can produce a usable golf club—if the shaft is poor quality the finest head and grip cannot turn it into a good club.

Two general rules worth considering are that the stronger or faster the swing the stiffer the shafts should be and I would have to say that many golfers would benefit from lighter clubs than the ones they normally play. The advances in lightweight shafts have made it possible to reduce the overall weight of clubs while still retaining enough weight in the clubhead to give the necessary amount of feel. It is this question of feel which is so important. It is an intensely personal thing and all the modern technology and computerised research which goes into golf club design these days means nothing if the club does not feel right in your hands.

What I would suggest, if you are not entirely satisfied with your present clubs, is that you experiment with a wide variety. Try a few shots with test clubs from your pro and get your golfing friends to let you try their clubs. It is only by trying something different that you will be able to find the elusive formula which suits you best.

Advances in equipment design

There is so much happening in golf design and development that you really owe it to yourself to experiment. The heel-toe weighting principle is now fairly universally used by manufacturers and it certainly seems to benefit the average golfer. By taking weight from the centre of the club blade and spreading it more towards the heel and the toe the manufacturers have managed to increase the impact point on the club face. This enlarged 'sweet spot' means that there is a larger contact area on the clubface from which the average player can achieve good results. Those who have trouble in getting the ball into the air have found the new low-profile clubs a great help. As their name suggests, these clubs have extremely narrow blades and the weight is concentrated towards the bottom. They certainly do seem to get the ball up very quickly.

Having found the right equipment to help you take the best advantage of your game, do spend a little time and effort on looking after it. I am a great believer in clean clubs, clean shoes and a clean white ball giving you the best chance to play well. Scruffy equipment and personal appearance can so easily lead to scruffy play. The right mental attitude can be created by the right appearance.

In wet weather keep a towel tied inside your umbrella. It will stay dry and give you a chance to wipe your hands and the grips of the clubs before each shot. After a wet round of golf remove the headcovers from your woods, wipe the clubs and allow the headcovers to dry separately. Don't leave your woods encased in wet covers for a week before your next game. Unless you can keep your left-hand glove dry you are usually better off without one in really wet conditions.

Taking care of your clubs is a simple job. One of the easiest ways is to have a small towel on your golf bag so that you can wipe the club after every shot. Always hit a clean golf ball with a clean club—you owe yourself nothing less.

Index

References in italics are to illustrations.